Sometimes
God Has
a Kid's Face

Letters from Covenant House

Bruce Ritter

Covenant House
1988

DEDICATED

to the thousands
of good and brave and beautiful
bought and sold kids
who never make it back
because no one reached out
to them in time. . .

This book is a selection of letters taken directly from *COVENANT HOUSE: Lifeline to the Street*, published in 1987 by Doubleday and reprinted with the full and free cooperation of Doubleday.

Grateful acknowledgement to the following for permission to quote from song lyrics in this book:

"Do You Know the Way to San Jose?" by Burt Bacharach and Hal David. Copyright © 1968 Blue Seas Music, Inc. and Jac Music Co., Inc. Used by permission. All rights reserved.

Contents

INTRODUCTION

Even Now It Hurts
to Write About It

In the almost 20 years of our existence we have tried our best to help the more than 100,000 kids we have taken off the streets into residence in our programs. We believe that we have been able to help about one-third make it back.

The rest? I think most of them don't make it. They die young. Or they go to jail, or join the tragic throngs of emotionally racked, alcoholic, and drugged inhabitants of what is becoming a vast and barely human national shelter system.

Kids don't survive very long on the street — at least in any recognizably human way. The distortion of the personality, the erosion of character are swift and massive and almost always irreversible.

More than 30 years ago, in 1956, in Rome, I was ordained a priest of the Roman Catholic Church as a member of the Franciscan Order. I have never wanted to be anything else. I certainly didn't know at the time that I would wind up in Times Square taking care of thousands of kids who had been bought and sold like so many potatoes.

The kids came into my life by accident. Or so I thought at the time. Ten kids who had no place to live, who had been pimped by a bunch of junkies, and who had been forced to make a porn film because they were hungry, just couldn't take it anymore and fled to my apartment in the slums of the Lower East Side of New York City.

I didn't have the guts to kick them out and I couldn't find anybody else who wanted them, so I kept them. Or, as one of the kids gleefully chortled, "Bruce, we're going to give you a chance to own us, to be our father." Since, as you probably know, being a priest can get pretty lonely at times, I didn't mind it a bit. "It's like having your cake and eating it, too, Bruce," one kid said.

"What gives you the right to know me so well so soon?" I said.

I never forgot what happened to those first kids. Nor can I forget or overlook or keep quiet about what's happened to thousands of others of my kids who, because they needed food and shelter, or maybe some money, and always some love — or all of these things— took their clothes off in front of a camera and let somebody make a permanent record of their need and their shame. And forced them to smile and not to cry.

Even now it hurts to write about it.

BEN-AMI

I Didn't Do
Anything Special

"Bruce, this is Ernie.
We found him sleeping in a garbage can."

"How long will it be before you guys sell out? To money, power, ambition...? Will you sell out by the time you're 25?"

I finished my sermon on that note and turned back to the altar to continue the celebration of Mass. I was proud that almost 400 students had come to church that brilliant Saturday afternoon in October 1966.

It was a good sermon. I liked that sermon. I had worked hard on it. It was all about zeal and commitment and how the students at Manhattan College should be more involved in the life and work of the Church.

One of the students, Hughie O'Neill, stood up in church and said, "Wait a minute, Bruce." He happened to be the president of the student body and captain of the track team.

"Bruce," he said, "you're making two mistakes. The first mistake you're making is that we are not going to sell out by the time we're 25; we'll undoubtedly do so by the time we're 21. Your second mistake, and your biggest one, is that you're standing up there telling us this instead of leading us by your example and lifestyle.

"We all think you're a pretty good teacher, Bruce, but we don't like your sermons. We think you should practice what you preach."

That's a pretty heavy shot to take from your students on a Saturday afternoon. (There was a general murmur of agreement from the other kids in church.)

I thought about it a lot over the next few days, and realized, of course, that Hughie O'Neill was correct. The next Sunday, at all the Masses on campus, I apologized to the student body—for not edifying them—and asked my superiors and the archbishop for a new assignment: to live and work among the poor on the Lower East Side of Manhattan.

In May of 1968, on Holy Thursday, I moved off campus and found an apartment in the East Village—on East Seventh Street near Avenue D. A couple of junkies had just been busted so I was able to take over their tiny three-room apartment. Me and 10 million cockroaches. The bathtub was in the kitchen which made it handy for washing dishes. The toilet was in the hallway.

Most of my neighbors were junkies, dealers and speed freaks. In fact, of the 72 apartments in my tenement at least half were occupied by junkies. For the first couple of months my neighbors left me completely alone—they thought I was a narc (an undercover narcotics agent) trying to get evidence on the drug scene.

Since I had no specific ministry—my assignment was simply to be useful to the poor—I became

involved in all the problems you'd expect to find if
you lived and worked in a slum: the poverty, the
violence, the drug scene, the unemployment, the
police corruption that was rampant in New York
City in the 60s.

I had no intention of becoming involved with
the kids of the neighborhood.

For almost a year I worked at anything and
everything I could find. My expenses were low. My
rent was $60 a month! My ministry to the poor didn't
seem to be getting anywhere, but I was pretty con-
tent. I figured that God would mess around in my life
again.

I became involved with the kids of the neighborhood quite by accident—and, quite frankly, against
my will.

One night, at 2 a.m. of a bitter day in February
1969, six kids knocked on my door. It was very cold
and snowing very hard and the four boys and two
girls looked half frozen. They were quite young—
all 16 and under—and asked if they could sleep on
the floor my apartment.

What could I do? It was snowing outside and
cold. What would you have done? I invited them
inside, gave them some food and blankets and the
kids bedded down on my living room floor. One of
the boys looked at me. "We know you're a priest," he
said, "and you don't have to worry. We'll be good
and stay away from the girls." I thanked him for that
courtesy!

The next morning it was still very cold and still
snowing very hard. The kids obviously did not want
to leave. They had no place to go. The girls got up

and cooked my breakfast and burned it; the boys cleaned my apartment and cased it.

One boy went outside for just a few minutes and brought back four more kids. "This is the rest of us," he said, "the rest of our family. They were afraid to come last night. They wanted us to check you out first. I told them that you didn't come on to us last night so that it was probably okay."

These 10 kids had been living down the block in one of the abandoned buildings with a bunch of junkies who were pimping them. The junkies had just forced the kids to make a porn film before they would give them some food. The kids hated that. They really hated that. In disgust and a kind of horror at the direction their lives were taking, they fled the junkies and came down the street to my place.

I tried very hard to find some child care agency that would take these kids in. I called over 24 different agencies.

Nobody would touch these kids.

Finally, in desperation, I called a very high official in the child welfare system and told him about the 10 kids sleeping on my floor. He told me about all the laws I was breaking. I was guilty of harboring and contributing to the delinquency of a minor, probably of interstate commerce in minors, and of a crime I had never even heard of before: the alienation of affection of children—which means that if the kids began to like me enough, they wouldn't want to go home again— and that's a crime in New York!

"Look," he said. "You've destroyed your reputation. There's only one reason people will think you've taken kids off the street. You've got to have them arrested. That's the only way to get them into care."

I couldn't do that. That wasn't the agreement I had made with the kids. So I kept them.

I got some old bunk beds and the kids moved off the floor into beds.

I really liked these kids. They were great kids!

The problem was the next day two more kids came in, and then the day after that two more. The word got around fast. You see my kids were telling other kids that I was a pretty good cook, there were no rats in the apartment, and that if they knocked on my door, I wouldn't have the guts to kick them out. They did, and I didn't.

One day my kids (right from the start I began to think of them as "my kids") brought me another kid and they said to me, "Bruce, this is Billy. He's 16. He's been living in a car for a year."

Every day, in order to keep warm, Billy would break into a car, jump-start the motor so he could run the heater and play the radio. If the cops chased him, or the owner, Billy would walk around the block, break into another car, jump-start the motor, play the radio. . . He survived that way for more than a year, panhandling, hustling.

I remember another scruffy kid they brought me. "Bruce, this is Ernie. He's 12. We found him sleeping in a garbage can." And they would look at me.

What could I do? What could anybody do? What would you have done? You would have taken them in, of course. I didn't do anything special.

Grab Him Back With Love and He Will Let You Go

You always own somebody you know that well, love that much.

At our regular weekly house meeting last Monday I talked to our kids about what it means to be part of a "covenant." The word has an ancient and sacred history—it goes back thousands of years and refers to a really solemn pact or agreement between persons to commit themselves to each other, to honor, respect, support and love each other.

The covenant we have with each other, I explained endlessly—having a congenital tendency to run off at the mouth—means we are sworn to love and care for them, and if they want us to, to own them. We want and expect the same back from them.

I saw four pairs of eyes dart around the room suspiciously. The other kids played it cool. I hastened on: Your primary obligation with us is to try to be happy and human. One kid snorted unbelievingly (but not cynically; I think he really wanted to hope it was true). I haven't been happy since the day I was born, Bruce.

Looking a gaggle of blighted tough-as-nails street kids smack in the eye and telling them they

have an obligation to love you back takes a certain
amount of guts. Maybe just not to street kids either;
maybe to say it to anyone. Anyway, they didn't
laugh, probably because I scowled menacingly as I
said it.

September 1972

He was a street kid, 16, long and skinny, eaten
by hunger and lice, bones and lungs rattling, scowl-
ing-weak and desperate from too many months on
pizza and Coke and acid and loneliness. Dark,
opaque eyes looked at nothing and missed nothing.

Infinitely armored (a knife, a club and piece of
taped pipe carefully stashed under pillow and mat-
tress), he mistrusted clean sheets and underwear,
showers, doors, windows, people, food, words,
eyes. Infinitely vulnerable, he could only eat and
sleep and eat, crouch, huddle, and posture before the
TV, letting himself be absorbed into the benign
world of the children's cartoons. I heard him break
silence after three weeks — a harsh, humorless bark-
ing guffaw, deliberate and calculated. I think he
wanted to assure me he liked it here.

Afraid, like most street kids, of place and space,
he didn't really settle in so much as gingerly occupy
the premises, always tentative in his acceptance of
the fact that it was his bed, his room. After the first
month he gave me his club, and then a few weeks
later his iron pipe. I had to wait six months for his
knife.

The breakthrough, when it came, was massive.

One of us — afraid, too busy, too tired, impatient — rejected him. Snarling and ugly he went to his room and sat on his chair, folding his hands tightly in his lap. He began to cry, harder and harder. After a while he could not sit on the chair anymore and he fell on the floor, curled fetus-like for two hours, straining out a grief he couldn't name.

The visible change that began then was wrenching for us all. He began to grow up all over again, and like a small child needed to touch and feel things and persons: us, our alarmed visitors, our kids. Always with a scowl, a threat of violence, the bleak opaque stare, always at the door to block your path, pin your arms, take your keys, your books, your cigarettes, records. I said that if he grabs you, why, grab him back with love and he will let you go and run away.

Testing us incessantly, he pushed out our limits. We had always to find new resources and new understanding. He tried one, then two jobs and failed, and acted out his discouragement with violence, rejecting us and our covenant for the cruelty and exploitation of the street scene. Shattering confrontations with me and Dave and Dan drove him back to the street. He returned a month later, sick, sadder, more understanding.

We found him another job, in a day-care center — five hours a day letting two- and three-year-old children climb on him, wet him, punch and grab him, love him and need him. He stopped grabbing us and punching us; he stopped, mostly, the blank, hard stares and became capable, more and more, of human speech, conversation.

We own him. I think for good, in the sense that you always own somebody you know that well, love that much. Covenant becomes a need after a while and it is no longer possible to say if it is his need or your need. It goes beyond the certain conviction he still has a long way to go, and that still, maybe, he won't make it. He has now a need for his own space and place to grow in. To grow away from us, to become independent of us and free of us.

June 1973

Kids come to Covenant House because they have no place to go. Most are in flight from deplorable living situations, hungry, and very scared. Some are in flight from themselves. The problem is, for all of them, very simple: Where am I going to sleep tonight? Or eat tonight? Who will take care of me tonight?

In a much deeper and totally unromantic sense the question is even more searing: Who will love me and care about me? Why doesn't someone? Sometimes the answer is devastatingly frank and brutal: Because we can't. Because you won't let us. Because you do bad things to people.

Paul was 16 and a thief with a real natural-born talent for thievery that he cultivated assiduously. He stole everything and anything—a turnip the cook was going to serve for dinner, wallets and radios and money, your socks and keys. (Paul had a special fondness for keys.) He stole every day, and the more he liked you the more he had to steal from you. We all liked him, too.

Having Paul for your friend was a real drag. Periodically he would beam at us all and proudly announce to his unwilling victims at Covenant House that he had managed to cut down on his stealing.

It got so bad one week that the other kids, in desperation, came to me and demanded that something be done before Paul got himself killed by an angry posse being formed in our living room. They wanted his blood bad, and intended to stretch his neck from the nearest fire escape. It was a real crisis. I wondered out loud whether I should throw Paul out, and my kids, in real disgust (remembering, maybe, their own past derelictions), said no, of course not, but that I had to do something, anything. We talked it over for a long time and I announced my decision.

Paul would be called before the entire staff, warned for the last time, and asked to undergo a retraining and purifying process: Everything would be removed from his room except his bed. He would be given a large blanket, and, in exchange, he would give us all his clothes, particularly the ones he was wearing. For two weeks Paul had to live in his blanket—and having nowhere to go, and especially no pockets, would be unable to steal anything. The only promise I could make to Paul was that sure death awaited any kid who stole his blanket. If Paul couldn't agree to this procedure, he had to leave.

I gave him five minutes to make up his mind and watched incredibly large tears roll down his cheeks.

He went to his room and we all waited, afraid. Ten minutes later, Paul returned, swathed in a blanket, cheating only a little—he had kept his underwear. We demanded that, too.

For two weeks, Paul lived in his blanket. Not once did any other kid bother him. Not once did he steal. After two weeks we ceremoniously gave him back his underwear, and, a week later, his shirt. Still no stealing. Another week and we gave him back his pants—and waited anxiously. Nothing happened. We returned his shoes and socks and restored him to full membership in our covenant. He didn't steal for almost three months. And then it happened. Paul fell off the wagon, hard. He went on a perfect binge—an orgy of stealing—anything, everything, from anybody, all the time, and we had to ask him to leave.

Paul has been away nine months, sadly, but relievedly, missed by all. He appeared out of nowhere the other day. He wants to come back and has no other place to go. Who would want a sticky-fingered, larcenous and large-pocketed walking vacuum cleaner around to suck up your possessions? The staff happily assumes that I am going to say yes. Things have been getting pretty quiet around here, I guess. Do you think I should greet Paul with a hug first and then his blanket, or vice versa? I mean, it's really dangerous to get close to that kid if he has pockets.

Smelling How Bad You Smell Can Take Your Voice Away

"Keep on doing what you're doing," the doctor said. "When you stop doing it, he will die."

January 1974

Last week, at two in the morning, somebody called us. They had found this kid that wouldn't talk wandering around. Tall, 17 maybe, blond. Really dirty. A coat at least six sizes too big drooped over a pair of pants so ragged and torn that he was two threads and a rip away from being naked. He smelled pretty bad.

He couldn't tell us anything except that he was from Washington. He was scared and his face had gone slack (hunger maybe). He couldn't walk straight, either — just graceful wooden Pinocchio-like lurches. All the kids stayed away from him. That's a really bad sign. Kids read kids pretty well.

Preliminary diagnosis: mild schizophrenia, mildly retarded. Gut reaction: hungry, lost, exhausted, panicked, hopeless, a nobody in a nowhere, no place. No place to start from to pass Go. We cleaned him up, gave him some underwear, a pair of pants, food. He didn't talk. Just sat on the couch without moving anything except his eyes. I stopped over at our crash pad the next morning to see how he was doing. He was still sitting on the couch, with a couple of other kids.

"Hey, you came in yesterday!" I didn't give him a chance to answer but began talking to the kid sitting next to him. A couple of minutes later I walked past him again. "You're from Washington," I said, and walked away before he could answer, circled back, said I was glad he had some clean clothes, and walked away again to joke with another hairy-monster kid who wanted to be joked with. Then I came back, stepped on his foot just a little, said I was really glad he was here, and walked over to the stove to stir the mashed potatoes.

The boy got up, walked over to the stove, and bumped into me, except that he didn't move away. We stood there, his right side to my left side, foot, calf, thigh, hip, shoulder pressed together. I stirred the carrots and peas, said I hoped he was hungry, and moved over to the broiler to check out the hamburgers.

The boy walked around the table and into me, bumping me, and did not move away, his left side to my right side: foot, calf, thigh, hip, shoulder pressed together. I stuck a fork in the hamburgers, pronounced them ready, said it was great having him around, punched him on the arm, and went back to my office.

The boy never said a word. I never heard his

voice. But he communicated superbly well. I went back yesterday. He was sitting on the couch, moving only his eyes. When he saw me he got up, walked over to the table, and set up a chessboard, arranging all the pieces. He didn't say a word. I have still never heard him speak. Maybe tomorrow.

A true story, word for word. You interpret it. Fear, exhaustion, loneliness (especially that), hunger, smelling how bad you smell, can take your voice away and unhinge your face, keeping only your eyes alive.

We have a lot of kids and lot more who want to come live with us. Help us, please. Thank you for sharing our conviction that children should not have to suffer.

October 1974

Let me tell you about Timmy. Of all my kids he's the one I love the most. He's not supposed to be a sophomore in college, getting all As and Bs. He's supposed to be dead. Four years ago his older brother brought him up the stairs to my apartment. Timmy could barely walk. He was 16, a five-foot-10-inch, 110-pound, black-haired, blue-eyed speed freak who had left a comfortable middle class home when he was 13 to wander and drift up and down the East Coast, wherever fancy and an incessant need for drugs would pull him.

Timmy lived any way he could, anyplace he could, pouring his life out daily through the hollow point of a needle. He swallowed or shot up anything he could find. (Once, almost in disbelief, he described how when he couldn't cop any drugs at all, he and a friend injected oven cleaner into their veins.)

I would wake Timmy every morning. He was crashing, depressed, semi-comatose from the speed he had obtained the day before, too weak and lethargic to move. I had to pull him up to a sitting position on the bed and sometimes, even swing his feet out onto the floor. Sometimes I would hand him his socks and pants and shirt, and sometimes because he just couldn't do it, I would have to dress him and haul, push, and cajole him to the breakfast table and make him eat. He would put five and six teaspoons of sugar into his coffee. (Speed freaks lust after sugar.)

On that quick energy Timmy would leave the apartment, cop some speed, shoot up, and come back flying, excited, energetic, happy, smiling, ecstatic — only to crash and collapse six to eight hours later in a puddle of profound misery and hopeless depression.

We surrounded him, as much as we could, 24 hours a day. We planned our own days to include Timmy. If Jerry had to go shopping, Timmy went along, and then Jerry would hand him over to Mike, who needed company while he picked up the laundry, who gave him to Bruce, who needed company on a trip to Manhattan College, who gave him to Pat and Adrian across the street, who fed him and made him laugh, who gave him to Mary, who wanted to

read a book with him, who gave him back to Jerry
and Bruce, who would make sure he was in his half
of the bunk bed in cockroach heaven.

We all lived this way for a couple of months,
Timmy and I and my friends. Timmy would always
escape to cop some speed. One night he came home,
gave me a bright-eyed, all-teeth-showing, infinitely
sad glass smile, went into his room and swallowed
30 sleeping pills. We and he were lucky, or blessed
by God, rather. He didn't die, though he wanted to.
We redoubled our efforts, placing Timmy in a pro-
tective human cocoon. He always escaped us.

In desperation I took Timmy for evaluation and
examination to one of the major New York medical
centers, where a research program in methadrine
(speed) addiction was being carried out. Over a
period of two weeks they gave him every test possible in their huge ultramodern facility and then
asked me to come for their diagnostic conference.

There were seven doctors, psychiatrists, psy-
chologists, and social workers present. The eminent
doctor leading the conference stated that in all his
experience he had never encountered any boy who
had so heavily abused so many different kinds of
drugs. He asked the other experts to offer their own
evaluation and prognosis of what was, in their judg-
ment, the possibility of survival. On a scale of one
to 10, they all gave Timmy zero chances to make it.
Very upset and shaken, I thanked them all and ap-
pealed to them for help: What can we do for Tim?
The doctor simply said, "Keep on doing what you

are doing. When you stop doing it, he will die."

Thanksgiving 1974

Tim didn't know the doctors said he was sup-posed to die. I never told him. It didn't matter much. He had already decided, chosen, wanted to, knew he would. My friends and I were afraid to stop trying to hold Timmy away from the edge of the cliff in his mind — we loved him too much. We continued to surround him for as many as the 24 hours every day that we could.

Little by little, it began to happen. As the weeks passed, for one whole day even, Timmy would not shoot up some speed. And then it was three entire days without drugs, and then, incredibly, a whole week! We celebrated. Timmy said to me that night with an indescribable look of hope that I can still see on his face, "You know, Bruce, I think I might live."

It was getting along toward summer in that year, and I was afraid to keep Tim with me during the long, hot, boring days in the East Village — drugs were as available as candy and cigarettes. Some Franciscan friars of my Order who knew Timmy's story took a deep breath, took a chance, and took him to their summer camp in the Adirondacks.

We expected the worst but it didn't happen. Tim didn't touch a thing for three months. He chopped wood, painted, learned to water ski, and discovered a close affinity with the forest and moun-tains and lakes. He also gained 30 pounds and grew some muscles for the first time in his life. I went to visit Tim in August. He was waiting for me on the dock, unashamedly prancing and leaping about, flexing his biceps. His face and eyes were intensely alive and he was bursting with pride. I never loved him so much as then

I had a surprise all cooked up for Tim when he came back to the city: his senior year in high school. Some really great Christian Brothers who run one of the best high schools in New York took a flier on him. Brother Kevin and his staff gave Tim enormous support and encouragement, forcing his mind to come back out of the shadows and start working again.

He's a sophomore in college now. It wasn't easy. Tim went through a lot of bad times: discouragement, just getting tired of being good. He got through it, though, and is getting As and Bs, talking of a career as a marine biologist.

Most of my kids don't make it. For every Tim there are a dozen or 20 Johns, Marks, Marys, Bills, Cindys, who never come in out of the darkness, who can't tear free from their vices . . .

My friends and I are grateful for Tim. He's taught us never to give up on a kid too easily.

Tim has taught me a lot about God, too. I've told Timmy a hundred times that God is the reason he made it back, because God loved him that much and wouldn't let him go. Tim believes it. Kids like Timmy are a good reason to be grateful on Thanksgiving.

That's How
the Game Is Played

He sat there, inspecting my jugular
with the guileless eye of the corrupted young.

May 1976

In the jargon of the street he's known as "rough trade," and he plies his wares, himself, up and down the Minnesota Strip. He is 15 and looks 18, and he's seen the elephant.

We faced each other across my desk, casually, relaxedly, while I carefully arranged my face and my eyes and my mind so that nothing I said or did or thought or felt for the next hour was spontaneous or unconsidered. He offhandedly, with the practiced skill that needed no explanation, probed for my weaknesses, inspecting my jugular with the guileless eye of the corrupted young. Slow waves of depravity and innocence washed in shadows of darkness and light across his face.

He used the shreds of his innocence with a kind of detached, hapless malevolence to evoke my sympathies. By turns he was cynical and callous, winsome and desperate—for knowing moments at a time, vulnerable. He drifted in and out of reach, in and out of touch, constantly probing, watching for the moment of advantage.

The Minnesota Strip is the slimy underbelly of Manhattan, a 15-block stretch of Eighth Avenue porno parlors, strip joints, pizza places, cheap bars, fleabag hotels, and thousands of drifters, hookers, and pimps. It parallels Times Square and intersects that block on 42nd Street, where a dozen third-rate movie houses crowd together in grimy brilliance. At night, the crowds of castoffs and nomads and derelicts mingle with the crowds of affluent theatergoers from the high-rent districts and suburbs. A lot of kids go there and make their living there. Like the boy across my desk.

You don't say very much to kids like that. It's always much more a thing of vibes and perceptions and boundaries. The trick is to offer what he needs at the moment, and rarely is that a lot of God talk. It's enough if he knows why you do it. This kid's needs were simple enough: a place to live, some safety, some food. What complicated the essentially simple immediacy of it all was our "no strings" thing. He wanted to pay for it. That's what he always had to do. That's how the game is played.

We play the same game with God all the time. We don't like his "no strings" love for us either, particularly if the "us" includes a depraved innocent, a vomit-spattered derelict, or a pimp with a stable of children whom he rents by the hour. We try desperately to climb up out of the us by being good, by being better, by deserving more.

We demand that God love us because we are good, and we are good to make God love us. We have to pay for it. That's the way we've always played the game. And to know that God loves us not because we are good, but to make us so, is sometimes unbearable. Because as he loves us, so we have to love us, all of us.

And so I try to love the kid across my desk in a way he really can't understand at all. But grace does, and God working in a depraved and empty and terrified heart does, and maybe, just maybe, the innocence will return to that face and he will take his eyes off my jugular and stop pushing his toe into my foot under the desk. Maybe that child who was never a child will become like a child. Maybe.

He is yours and mine. Like it or not, he is part of us.

June 1976

triage (tre azh) F, sorting. . . , to pick out 1.
        Brit; a) the process of grading market-
        able produce b) the lowest grade of
        coffee berries consisting of broken ma-
        terial. 2) the sorting of and treatment of
        battle casualities at the front. . .
        WEBSTER'S THIRD NEW INTERNATIONAL DICTIONARY

Surgeons separate the wounded into three categories: the slightly wounded would recover no matter what you did, those so severely injured that medical help was useless, and the other seriously wounded that might live if helped immediately. The first two kinds were left unattended and uncared for.

I met Peter five years ago when he was 14—a street kid—and hadn't seen him for over a year when he walked into my office yesterday. He was wearing skin-and-muscle tight brief cut-offs and a body shirt unbuttoned to the waist. We exchanged greetings—mine delighted, surprised, his muted and detached.

I hoped he was doing well. Peter gave a sad, wry smile. "Okay," he said. "Not bad," he said. "I think of killing myself a lot," he said.

"Do you need a place to stay?" I said.

"No," he said. "I stay at the Continental Baths. It's cheap. I kind of help out around there."

"It's a bad scene," I said.

"It's a living," he said. And then I think he remembered about dying because he started slightly, sat for just an instant of frozen immobility, then shrugged, and again gave me a faint, sad smile.

"Come back to Covenant House, Pete."

"No more programs, Bruce. I'm too old. I'm a male hustler, Bruce. I'm not gay. I'm bisexual..." He stopped and his face twisted. He couldn't continue.

"Come on back, Pete, to our school. We'll get you a job. That lifestyle is going to kill you, Pete. It's rotten that you have to do that." He didn't hear me. I grabbed his hand, his arm. "We've got this really great place on Third Street, Pete—really good people."

He looked at me in great pain. "I'm a go-go boy,

Bruce, in this bar on Second Avenue. I dance there. If the johns like me they stick a $5 bill in my jock strap."

"Come back, Pete We'll find you a place. It's not too late, Pete. This Monday, Gene, downstairs, will get you a job. He's an expert at it. It's okay, Pete. I'm really glad you're back."

"Bruce, I'm a stripper in a male burlesque joint: four performances a night for a hundred bucks. I dropped out of school in the seventh grade. I worked a couple of girls for a while, Bruce."

He couldn't stop. He had to tell me the whole sad, sick story. It was almost as though he was afraid to leave out any details, like when you go to confession. I went on patting his hand.

"I'm really glad you're back, Pete. So are Gretchen and Steve and Dave. You've got to change your lifestyle, Pete. You're into a lot of things that make you feel pretty sick about yourself."

"Bruce, I don't have any clothes. All my stuff was ripped off. I had a stereo. . ."

"Pete, you're not going to get out of that mess you're in without help."

"There's a warrant out for my arrest, Bruce. I pawned a gold bracelet for a friend. It turned out to be stolen."

"We can work that out, Pete. We've got a place for you and a job and school. We've missed you a lot, Pete."

Finally there was no more to tell; the small dirty puddle that was his young life spilled out between us.

He relaxed and took a deep breath. "I think I'll go downstairs and talk to Gene about that job. Is it okay if I come back and talk to you again on Monday?" He looked down at his hot pants with some amusement. "I can't go for an interview in these."

Pete can make $400 a week, tax-free, on the street. It's going to be pretty tough for him to work 40 hours a week for $2.50 an hour. It's going to be even harder for him to go back to school and learn how to read and write. He's a good kid. He came in to see me for a lot of reasons he didn't really understand very well.

He's not a Catholic and not a religious kid and he doesn't know anything about going to confession, but he needed and wanted absolution bad. Like most of us, he was about as sorry as he could be.

A lot of people drift into, slide and choose into a lifestyle that ultimately kills them. It might be too late for Pete. The Peters of this world are refuse in our social sewers, to be inexorably flushed down and out, drowned in a sea of garbage, human pollution to be coped with and buried and dumped. Many honest, caring people think so.

One such, a good friend, sighed and murmured the word "triage." Let them go, Bruce. Think of the others, the ones you know you can help, the ones that still have a chance. He's already almost dead, Bruce.

Peter is already almost dead, and I think maybe the one way he feels he can reassert some control over his life is to end it. Pete is most definitely one of the Lord's lost sheep. He is not the white, cuddly, innocent lamb that just happened to wander away from the fold. In biblical categories I think it fair to say that Pete is a sinner, the kind over which heaven rejoices if they turn away from their evil and turn back to God. Pete can't do that without God's help, nor can we.

Pete doesn't really want to end his life, but he's not certain he can begin it again either. Only the Lord can provide the massive life-support systems he needs to make it, and—to carry through with the metaphor—places like Covenant House must exist as the intensive care units for these dying children.

July 1976

It was two in the morning, and I couldn't get back to sleep because someone was pounding on the door. When I opened it, there were two kids standing there, 14 and 15 maybe. "Are you Bruce?" the one asked.

"Yes," I said.

"Do you take kids in?"

I looked at the bodies lined up on the floor. "Yes," I said.

"Can we stay with you?" he asked, hesitating.

"No," I said. "We have no room."

He started to cry. "What can we do, where can we go?" he said.

"You can go back out into the street and look sad," I said.

He stopped crying. "I can do that," he said, his eyes never leaving my face. I never saw them again.

1976 — 1979

The X-rated Children

"Take this one," he said.
"You'll like this one.
His name is Nandy. He's 11."

August 1976

I live on the Minnesota Strip — Eighth Avenue between 43rd and 44th Street. It's a sick, festering pus-filled boil of a place where the corruption and violence and exploitation of a diseased society burst into the open. You can find all the sadness in the world here.

I left my place yesterday morning at 7:30 to go down to my Covenant House office. I stepped over a puddle of vomit in the doorway, said good morning to the prostitutes hanging out there, and walked down 42nd Street to the Seventh Avenue subway.

There was a blond kid, about 15, leaning against the wall of a porno movie theater. Next to him was an overflowing garbage can. He gave me that unmistakably, speculative, inquiring look. The boy was still there when I passed back the same way at 6 p.m. There was a drunk stuffed in the garbage can.

I went out again around 2 a.m to get a bite to eat,

and stepped over the drunk in my doorway; there were 17 (I counted them) prostitutes across the street, moving slowly back and forth. It was a warm night, and the streets were crowded with hundreds of the night people, washing up and down the littered sidewalk. There was an indescribable sense of violence and electric tension, a fascination, the anticipation of something about to happen.

The boy was still there. We nodded at each other. I walked down 42nd Street and saw seven kids just hanging about by one of the porno book stores. The oldest was 16—obviously a runner for a pimp. (A runner is a kid who works for a pimp as a negotiator. Johns don't like to talk directly to pimps. They're afraid of pimps. It's easier to make the deal with a runner who will negotiate time, place, price...)

The older kid, the runner, touched me on the arm. "Which one do you want?" he said. "You can have any one you want for $20."

I said I wasn't into that, but he didn't believe me. He called over one of the kids. "Take this one," he said. "You'll like this one. His name is Nandy. He's 11."

Sermons on sin are usually abstract statements about abstract offenses against a God who is also conveniently abstract. Sin, in the concrete on Eighth Avenue and 42nd Street, is sin in the X-rated lives of children, in their X-rated eyes and X-rated faces and their X-rated bodies. The kids are sinners. We are too. But they are children who need finding and reaching out to.

They're good kids, mostly. They really are. When you're 14 and 15, and you can't read or write very well, and have no place to live, and it's cold and you're hungry and you have no marketable skills, you market yourself. They are children who desperately need help in an area where there are no services for them and where there's no place to go for help.

That's why Covenant House plans to open a multi-service center on Eighth Avenue. It will be open 24 hours a day, seven days a week, and offer no-questions-asked help to any kid who needs a bed, food, safety, a way out from a degrading lifestyle. Jobs and school too and medical help and just comforting and self-respect, so the kid who hangs out by the porno theater won't have to make his living there anymore.

I've got this great place on Eighth Avenue, all kinds of space, including a church! And a residence, and a walk-in center and offices and stores. . .

I extend a serious invitation to anyone who would like to give a year of his life to the Lord and to work with us and the kids on Eighth Avenue. We can provide free room and board and pocket money and insurance and a chance to practice the corporal and spiritual works of mercy.

This religious commitment is not only a survival mechanism — which it surely is — but also an indispensable means of bringing the Lord's grace and presence into the lives of these kids. . .

America's "Untouchables"

He had a warm, open smile.
"Hi," he said. "My name is Larry.
I sell people."

August 1977

There's a mystery here, in this story, of grace and sin. I wish I understood it better than I do. Let me tell you what happened so you can try to understand it too. I never met him, although he tried several times to see me, just dropping over, taking a chance I'd be in the center and I never was. My staff tells me he's a big man, inches over six feet. A couple of times he sent over runaway girls too young to work for him, and once a really sick youngster.

He owns and operates the newest and raunchiest peep show and brothel in town, just across the street: beautiful girls — 25 cents a look. Over a dozen prostitutes work the place. (Average time with a john is seven to 20 minutes. For $20.) The place is open about 18 hours a day.

Last week, at about three in the morning he came over again, carrying a milk bottle filled with quarters, dimes and nickels. "This is for your kids," he

said. "We like what you're doing. I'm in a bad
business but I don't like kids getting hurt. We
collected this money from my girls and their johns
for your kids." He handed the milk bottle filled with
money to Peter, the young and by now bug-eyed,
slack-jawed staff person on duty and walked away.
"God bless you," he said. It came to $84.20.

The next morning my staff told me what happened. I was furious. I was outraged. I also laughed
till I cried. "Take it back, right away," I said. "Tell
him no thanks. Thanks a lot, but no thanks. Tell him
we appreciate the thought but no thanks. Thank him
for sending the kids over though."

I thought that was the end of it, just a bizzare
incident to add to the many hundreds of others. But
he came back the next day dressed in a beautiful
white silk suit, grabbed a broom to help Peter sweep
the sidewalks. "He didn't have the right to do that,
that priest. He didn't have the right to refuse a gift
to God. I don't hurt anybody. I've got four kids. I
got to make a living. I cleaned up my place, made the
girls stop stealing and ripping off the johns. I go to
church. I tithe. I gave the money to another church."
He went back across the street, got into his gold
Eldorado and drove away.

The more I thought about it, the more the inex-
plicable mystery of sin and grace and love, of lying
and caring, oppressed and obsessed me. I think he
tried to do a good thing. Yet what he does across the
street is clearly evil. "God bless you," he said. He
gives 10 percent of his "income" to charity. He runs

a low-class brothel and cares about runaway kids and people who help them. And he wanted very much to be understood.

I can't get that "God bless you" out of my mind. I couldn't have said it back to him; the words would have stuck in my throat. I hate what he does. I'd do my best to close him down. But I have this awful suspicion that he was sincere. I wouldn't worry so much if he were quite clearly a flaming hypocrite. But that "God bless you" . . . I think he really meant it. And my mind reels and I can't understand.

I know a lot about mixed motives. I'm the world's expert on mixed motives — my own — trying to disentangle the good from the evil, to unravel the knotted skein of my better self. . . the weeds growing with the wheat . . . and suddenly I am overwhelmed by my kinship with this man, for we are both sinners hoping in the mercy of God and His forgiveness.

Thanksgiving 1977
There were two absolutely beautiful kids. Anna was a pretty little blonde 13-year-old from New England. Mike was 14, a good-looking kid from Delaware. They had some problems at home, but more than that, they wanted some excitement, some action! They wanted to stand near the edge of the cliff and look over; they were beautiful moths, flying, dipping, swooping around the bright lights and candles of the Minnesota Strip.

They were good kids, but kids, and they didn't

really know that guys like Larry existed. Steve and I met him one night down the street from our place, about 11:30. We had been out walking around, getting some fresh air and looking for kids and were standing just watching the crowds when he walked up to us.

He was tall, imperially slim, impeccably dressed. He had a warm, open smile. He shook our hands warmly. He looked us straight in the eye. "Hi," he said, "my name is Larry."

"I sell people," he said. "Would you like to come around the corner to my hotel? We have a suite on the fifth floor. We have a live male sex act first and then a live female act. We specialize in women: white, black, Spanish, Oriental. No sadomasochism," he warned, and gave us that disarming smile again. "Come around the corner," he said. "I'll take you in the first time, and then we make you a member of the club. We're open 24 hours a day, seven days a week. It's only $25 for half an hour." Steve and I said no. We were, shall we say, nonplussed!

In the meantime, back at the center, Anna and Mike were anxious to begin their new careers as cliff hangers and moths seeking candles to burn up in. Anna was approached by at least six pimps. We discouraged some.

Larry, who sells people, wanted and needed some new merchandise, and since he was too old to get into Under 21 he sent in a runner named Bobby to "get" Anna. Bobby was a smooth, fast-talking 18-year-old. We stopped him, too.

1979 — 1982

BEN-AMI

"Then They Sold Me to the Corporation"

*"I'd appreciate it
if you didn't lay any God talk on me."*

Marge had that special look on her face that warned me she meant business. "I think you ought to see this kid, Bruce." She said it with a no-nonsense deadly seriousness that was almost a command.

I always listen *very* carefully when Marge talks. At 61, she's the oldest member of our volunteer community, the resident grandmother of Under 21, and a very wise lady—with that special wisdom that comes from raising her own family right down to a passel of beloved grandchildren that she spoils outrageously. (She spoils my kids, too.)

"Sure," I said, "I'll go downstairs in a few minutes." It was about 9 p.m., the tag end of a very hard day, and I sure wasn't looking forward to another heavy conversation.

I never got that few minutes. Another member of our community just "happened" to come by my room. Peter, a summer volunteer, is 40 years younger than Marge and also blessed with a special wisdom about people. He is, I think, a very holy person. He hasn't learned to mask his feelings very well yet, and the urgent concern in his face alarmed me. "There's this kid in the center, Bruce. He's pretty bad off. . ."

I didn't waste any more time. I went downstairs to the center. "My name is Bruce," I said.

"I'm Mark," he said. "I'm from _____." He named a large southwestern city. "I saw you on *60 Minutes* and had to talk to you so I hitchhiked 2,000 miles. I was afraid to take a plane or bus." He was 19, a good-looking kid, with a lot of black hair falling over a pair of the most watchful blue eyes I had seen in a long time. A slender, coiled-spring body moved restlessly all the time we talked.

"I ran away when I was 14," he said. "My father and mother were alcoholics." Mark stopped for a moment and looked at me searchingly. "I've got to tell you this," he said, with a small rather uncertain smile. "If you don't mind, I'd appreciate it if you didn't lay any God talk on me."

He began again. "I met this guy. He gave me a lot of affection and a place to live. I needed the affection real bad. He taught me a lot about sex and, I guess, he put me to work. I didn't mind it so much after a while.

"I was young and pretty, so he sent me out to my customers dressed like a girl — a transvestite." His face twisted a bit. "I lived with 14 other boys in this big house. We were all pretty young, and pretty scared. He made all of us watch a kid get beaten, with a hanger. It was bad. That's what happened when you tried to leave. The next time you're dead."

Mark lit his 10th cigarette of the hour. His hands were shaking slightly. "When I turned 17 and got some muscles, and my beard began to grow, I went butch — I didn't have to wear girls' clothes anymore, and then I got old enough and they made me join another group, Man-to-Man. It was a call service. Pretty high-class customers. . ." His voice trailed off. "Then they sold me to the corporation."

I've never seen a kid look so desolate and forlorn. He suddenly appeared a lot older than 19.

"I had a company car and an apartment and took care of corporation clients. They would fly me all over the country. The corporation had a representative that would take a portfolio of the kids in their stable, both boys and girls, to their clients. We didn't have any clothes on in the photographs. The clients could pick anyone they wanted. I was pretty popular. . . They would come to my apartment."

Mark named the corporation. It's one of the Fortune 500. "I'm afraid," he said. "They don't like you to leave them. I left the car and just started hitchhiking. What can I do? I don't even know if you can help me, or would want to." His voice trailed off again. He tried not to cry, but couldn't manage it very well.

"I can help you a lot," I said. "Stay around for a while. We'll work something out." I took Mark over to Carl, who was supervisor on duty that night.

"This is Mark," I said. "Let him stay as long as he likes. Don't discharge him without seeing me." I grabbed Mark's hand and held it for awhile. "Just stay around," I said. "You'll be safe here. I'll talk to you tomorrow."

He was gone the next morning. Nobody knows where or why. Probably because he just couldn't trust anybody that much, that soon. I never got a chance to use any God talk on him. I pray a lot for Mark. I don't think he will come back.

February 1980

"A lady should never get this dirty," she said. She stood there with a quiet, proud dignity. She was incomparably dirty—her face and hands smeared, her clothes torn and soiled. The lady was 11. "My brothers are hungry," she said. The two little boys she clutched protectively were 8 and 9. They were two of the most beautiful children I've ever seen.

"Our parents beat us a lot," she said. "We had to leave." The boys nodded dumbly.

"We had to leave," one of them echoed. The children did not cry. After living on the street for two weeks they did not cry. I struggled to manage part of a smile. It didn't come off very well. The littlest kid looked back at me with a quick, dubious grin. I gave him a surreptitious hug. I was all choked up. "I would like to take a shower," she said.

I was over in our new center on 10th Avenue — the one Governor Carey gave us, God bless him — just checking things out, talking to the kids. It's brand new, you see, and the kids have only been in the place for a few weeks and they're still getting used to it. They like the new center a lot. What's more, they appreciate it.

A few minutes ago a kid who would never win any beauty prizes walked up to me, a typical Times Square hugger-mugger nomad, the kind you would never want to meet in a dark alley and the kind you'd like to have beside you if you had to walk down one. He was a big kid with lots of muscles hanging on him.

"Bruce," he said, "this is really nice," and he began patting me on the shoulder. "Thanks a lot," he said. "You must have a soft spot in your heart for us kids," and I said I did. And he said, "Bruce, why did you make it so beautiful?" And I said, "Because you're beautiful." And he smiled at me. I got more choked up — close to tears in fact.

I can't cry — it's bad for my image— so I was glad when another kid walked over and he punched me on the arm and he said he really liked the plants and the flowers, and his friend who came with him said it was better than the Holiday Inn, and then this little girl said, "Come see my baby, Bruce." He was six weeks old and lying in the middle of one of our comfortable lounge chairs. He was a cute little kid. She was 16.

The new center, I reflected ruefully, was a dream come true, and just maybe also the beginning of a nightmare. You see, we had decided to move the kids in by stages: to open our first dormitory of 50 beds, move the kids in, and then work out the programmatic kinks before we opened the other 60 beds. It made good sense to do it that way. The new dormitory is beautiful: small, attractive single rooms, really grand toilet and shower facilities, a comfortable lounge, a dream of a dining room — cafeteria-style.

We had over 70 kids sleeping on the floor in our Eighth Avenue Under 21 last Monday when we ceremoniously moved 50 kids over to the new dormitory. The kids were ecstatic, and I was relieved and happy. Not only because the kids had a new beautiful place to live in, but because there were just 20 or so kids left sleeping on the floor, and I was confident that in a couple of weeks — when God sent us enough money — I could open the other 60 beds.

Then something terrifying happened. In 24 hours another 50 homeless and abused youngsters appeared like magic and slept on that vacated floor. Now we have 120 kids instead of 70. I am scared that when we open our last 60 beds another 60 kids will appear out of the night and fill up the floor again. There's got to be an end to them. There's got to.

I thought back to a conversation I'd just had about an hour before with our director of finance, Bob Cardany. He came to my office trailing yards of computer printouts. The look on his face told me it was bad news.

"Bruce," he said, "do you know that we've spent our entire food budget for this fiscal year in the first five months? Did you know that? "We're way over the budget in all categories. We can't go on like this."

"I know," I said. "We have to."

"Where are we going to get the money?" he said.

"That's *God's* problem," I said.

Our problem is, of course, that we don't turn any kids away. I've told my staff that I'd fire them if they turned a kid away. I used to, before I knew better. When we just didn't have any more room I would say no. But I can't do that anymore. I know now, too well, what happens to a kid when he stays on the street.

So I've ordered my staff never to turn a kid away.

They must take them in. Regardless of how many knock on our door. So many kids come in every night now that I've had to tell my staff to sleep the kids in our chapel: the 10, 20, 30, 40 extra overflow kids will sleep on the floor of our chapel on Eighth Avenue on the Minnesota Strip under the altar, in the sanctuary, and the aisles.

When you think about it, a church is not a bad place to sleep kids in. The company is great, and besides, people have been sleeping in church for a long time, especially on Sunday!

Lent 1980

Benny is a pimp. He appeared at Under 21 just before midnight, all 200 hostile pounds of him, menacing, insistent. He wanted to see Julie, and right away.

Our supervisor, Winston, explained that Julie was upstairs asleep and didn't want to see him. Julie was 17 and wanted nothing to do with Benny. Benny got even uglier; he demanded to see her and tried to force his way in the door. Our staff stopped him. (I have a very gentle staff and quite a few of them are big and gentle. It took a lot of bigness to gentle Benny.)

Benny went berserk, screaming in rage and anger. "I spent a lot of money to put clothes on her back. It's time she got on her back and made me some money. I'm gonna come back here with a gun and blow you all away!"

Holy Week, 1980

Without preamble he launched into it: "Thanks, Bruce, for running this place. It helps a lot of kids. If this place had been around five years ago when I ran away (I was 13 then), maybe I wouldn't be where I am now. It's probably too late for me," he said, matter-of-factly. But then, almost as if the brutal finality of what he said was too much for him to bear, he continued without pausing for breath. "I've got to get my act together," he said.

I had stopped downstairs to have lunch with the kids — it's one way of keeping in touch — and I picked an empty chair at a table with a kid who hadn't quite completed growing up yet. "My name is Bruce," he said.

"Mine is too," I said.

He smiled. The kid was an almost tall, kind of

an almost finished kid, just under six feet. A cane hung on the back of his chair. Chicken pot pie was on the menu, and he made suitable compliments to our chef as I sat down.

"I live mostly on the subways," he said. "It's got so that I like the noise. Can't sleep anymore without lots of noise. My leg got hurt on forty-deuce. Stomped," he said. "I can't really work because of this leg. Never finished the sixth grade, although they kept passing me to the ninth grade although I wasn't never there. I can't read, Bruce. I would like to get a job, but I have to panhandle most of the day to get food money. I have to get my head together," he said.

Then something happened to his face that was absolutely terrifying. Something that went on inside and crawled out through the flesh, seeped through the skin around his mouth and eyes, mushing the dozens of tiny muscles that held his face together. "I don't like to hustle johns," he said. "Besides, it's harder now. I'm not so pretty anymore. I'm what they call rough trade, Bruce. Thanks for running this place. I'm 18," he said. "I'm going to get it together," he said.

The boy with my name understands very little about what happened in a grove of trees in a garden called Gethsemane, where the life of a man named Jesus fulfilled its cosmic purpose with a passion and fire and totality that we simply call the "Passion." I thought back to another conversation with another kid who understands a lot more about it.

"Hi," he said, "my name is Tommy. I'm from Indiana. I'm here to be a volunteer." He was a great looking kid.

"That's great," I said, "but you look awful young."

"I'm 18," he said, proudly and a bit apprehensively.

"That's awful young," I said. "How did you hear about Covenant House?"

"I read about it in the newspaper," he said. "I gave my boss two weeks' notice, quit my job and told my mother I was coming east to work on Eighth Avenue."

"How did she like that?" I said.

"Not very much," he said, "but anyway, my mom and dad gave me a farewell party, I got on a bus, and here I am."

"Why didn't you write or call or something?" I said (because if he had I would have said, "Thanks a lot but no thanks; you're too young.").

Tommy looked at me and he said, "I thought if I just came you would see that as a sign of faith in God."

What do you say to a kid like that? I said what we adults always say when we don't know what to say. I said, "We'll see." He's still here. A really super kid. A little young for this work maybe, but a super kid with great convictions.

"I Get $10 Apiece for You"

The word on the street is,
johns prefer chickens.

August 1980

Linda was 11, still a virgin, when her pimp took her. Peter was dancing on bars when he was 16. Martha was 14 when her pimp dyed her hair, got her a phony ID, and put her to work in a massage parlor. Tony was only 15 when he finally fled, in terror, Paul Abrams' call boy service. Annie was still only 15 when her pimp went to her mother's house in upstate New York, waited until her mother left for work, and took a very unwilling Annie back to life on the street and near death.

There are many reasons why we have a sex industry in Times Square—and now, all around the country. The simple, undeniable fact is that we want one. There are literally millions of customers— almost exclusively 100 percent male—who patronize this multi-billion-dollar business.

Millions of customers! Who choose to believe the bizarre myth that prostitution is a victimless crime. Who choose to believe that prostitution is

nothing more than a commercial recreational trans-
action between someone who wants to buy something and someone who wants to sell. Millions of
customers who choose to believe that sex is entertainment and that it's okay to pay the entertainers.
We have, in our liberated society, chosen to scoff at
the notion that there is something sacred and deeply
personal and profoundly private about sexual experience.

The sex industry here in Times Square is not
only geographically continuous with the entertainment industry (that great gathering of fine theaters
and restaurants that has justly won for Times Square
the title of entertainment center of New York City);
the sex business, dominated and controlled by organized crime, has actually formed a continuum
with the entertainment industry. It has almost become impossible to distinguish between some as-
pects of legitimate theater and the sex industry. And
we seem to want it that way.

If you wanted to spend a sophisticated evening
at the theater, and had $25 to spend, you could, for
your $25, buy a front row seat at *Oh! Calcutta!*, the
longest running (over 12 years) erotic musical in
New York. For your $25, in your front row seat, you
can watch a dozen young naked bodies, male and female, sing and dance and tell you jokes while they
simulate sodomy and intercourse on the stage.

If you don't have $25, but you do have 25 cents,
you can take your quarter down the block to the peep
show just down the street from Under 21 on Eighth

Avenue. You can drop your quarter in a slot, and for 90 seconds a screen will flip up, and you can watch one naked young lady dance. She won't sing. She will tell you some very filthy jokes, and she will invite you to masturbate.

There is no ethical or moral or qualitative difference between spending that $25 to see *Oh! Calcutta!* for your sophisticated evening at the theater, and spending that 25 cents at the peep show owned by members of organized crime, or watching the action at a West Side hangout on West 45th Street run by Matty "the Horse," or enjoying the entertainment at the Pussycat, another sexual supermarket owned and operated by Micky Zaffarano, the top pornographer of them all, located right in Times Square. It's just sex as entertainment, and very big business.

Hundreds of thousands of New Yorkers and out-of-town visitors patronize the sex industry and make a lot of very unwholesome people very rich. There's no mystery to why we have a sex industry. The reasons have always been the same: greed and lust. And our inability to care enough about what happens to the young people who, every year, become enslaved by the industry to satiate our appetites.

This year we expect at least another 10,000 beautiful kids to come through our doors. Most of them will have been involved, on some level, with the industry. Most of them call it making a few bucks. I have never met a young prostitute, girl or boy—and I've met hundreds—who wanted to be one. I've never met a young prostitute, girl or boy, who did not start out as a runaway.

One of my boys put it for me very directly. "Bruce," he said, "I've got two choices: I can go with a john (a customer) and do what he wants (His acutal phrase was "sell my tail."), or I can rip somebody off and go to jail. And," he said, "I'm afraid to go to jail. I wouldn't make it through my first shower. I can't get a job. I have no skills. I have no place to live." He is 16. I do not know what I would have done if I were 16 and faced with that impossible choice.

That's why we run Under 21, and that's why we keep it open 24 hours a day, to give these boys and girls a third alternative, an option that leads to life and not death.

You see, the word on the street is johns prefer chickens — kids. Because of greed and lust, and our sloth and fear. Who, after all, wants to take on organized crime? Our politicians certainly don't. Our law enforcement groups can give you a thousand reasons why they can't either. Our prosecutors and our judiciary tell us they have their hands tied. And everybody has a finger to point at the other guy.

Who wants to take on the well-organized, well-financed pressure groups that worry more about the civil liberties of pimps and criminals than those of their victims? Who wants to be held up to scorn and ridicule as book burners and fanatics because they see pornography as a degradation of an entire gender and a classroom for rape and seduction?

Maybe they're not the nice cuddly lambs that just happened to walk away from the fold, but they

are good kids. And, God knows, they are certainly
sinned against. They are also, God knows, the lost
sheep of the Gospel that Jesus said we must go out
and find; they are the prodigal sons not yet returned
to their fathers, the young Magdalenes not yet aware
of their need for forgiveness.

They're good kids. Not good maybe the way
your kids are good, and not nice maybe the way your
kids are nice. But good kids. What happens to them
should not happen.

September 1980

Unsavory, bum, derelict, malevolent, con artist,
raunchy, dangerous—were the words that, unbid-
den, and with surprising urgency, surged up out of
my memory banks. He had reached out a tentative
arm and stopped our slow progress up Eighth Avenue.

"Hi," he said, "my name is Jason." I groaned
inwardly and mentally scrubbed my mouth out with
soap, once again aware of how easy it was for me not
to see God in him. I wished for the hundredth time
that month that St. Francis had never embraced that
leper and wondered when I was ever going to grow
up and climb down out of my spiritual high chair.

It was about 10:30 on a warm, muggy, Times
Square night. The Democratic convention was in
full swing and New York was jammed with visitors.
The predators and jackals along the Minnesota Strip
were out in force stalking their game.

He spoke to us with that fawning candor older

street people use when they begin their hustle and seek to disarm their wary prey. We were, to Jason, just two slightly paunchy, bald and balding fiftyish out-of-town visitors looking for some action. My friend, another Franciscan priest, Father Douglas Lawson, from our headquarters in Union City, NJ, had come to visit.

"Would you gentlemen like to come to our place on 48th Street? It's just off Eighth Avenue." He paused. "I get $10 apiece if I bring you in."

"What's the place all about?" I said.

"It's a bar," he said. "Cheap drinks. Straight business. Live sex acts, lesbians, everything. You don't have to buy any girls. Just sit and watch if that's all you want to do. We have 12 girls to pick from — 14 to 21. Forty-five dollars for an hour, $60 for four hours, $100 all night. The girls have to do what you want," he said. "We have six places. We'll give you a membership card and you're welcome at any of them. They're run by _____." He mentioned his name. (You would know it if I said it.) "I get $20 if I bring you in," he said.

He followed us for almost a block, repeating his offers, making his pitch, selling his merchandise. Some of the merchandise was only 14 years old. "I get $10 apiece for you," he said.

It Doesn't Take Long
To Murder a Child

You become what you do,
and you no longer even care. . .

Sixteen-year-old Jenny watched the old yellow Cadillac with Texas plates drive slowly down the street in Baltimore. Classes in summer school were over for the day, and Jenny was waiting for a bus to take her home. "Want a ride, baby?" The two men and two women in the car seemed friendly.

"Sure, and thanks," she said, and threw her school books in the back seat and climed in. The date was July 9.

It happened that simply. Jenny, a really good kid, was on that day a not very smart kid. The car quickly turned north on Interstate 95 and headed toward New York City.

"Take me home. You've got to let me out. Stop the car," Jenny demanded. Lenny and Pat and Joe and Carol just laughed. " There's a $500 charge on you, baby," Lenny said. "You've got to work it off. Don't make us any trouble."

The yellow Caddie stopped at a couple of truck

stops on the way north. The incredulous schoolgirl, by now in a state of total shock, was forced to turn tricks with some truckers. Joe beat the reluctance out of her. Lenny kept the money.

The four adults, and by now benumbed child, arrived in New York City and checked into a seedy hotel on the Grand Concourse in the Bronx. Lenny and Pat and Joe and Carol split up. Jenny was forced to stay with Joe in the hotel. They changed rooms every day. Jenny was put out to work the streets in the Hunts Point section of the Bronx. (Hunts Point is the pits! There isn't any more dangerous, ugly place for a kid.)

Joe beat her a lot — Jenny was not a very willing and cooperative captive. She managed to escape in the middle of the night after Joe fell asleep. Jenny took $50 from his pants and grabbed a cab to Manhattan's Lower East Side. Exhausted and confused, she checked into another cheap hotel.

Jenny poured out her story to a young woman in the next room. Toya was sympathetic and understanding. "I'll help you, baby. Me and my friend, Blue Fly, next door."

Blue Fly is a really evil, rotten pimp. He laughed at the girl: "Your mistake, baby, was telling somebody your story. For being so dumb, I'm laying a $1,000 charge on you. You can work it off on the Bowery. Don't try to escape again. The police won't help, and we'll get you, we really will. There's no place you can hide."

Jenny tried to refuse to work and was beaten.

She didn't bring back much money and she was beaten again. The terrified kid decided that she had nothing to lose — being dead was better — and broke away and ran down the street, chased by Toya and Blue Fly. Jenny dived into a large parking lot, rolled under a car, and waited, panting convulsively, until Blue Fly and Toya ran past. Jenny got back on her feet in almost mindless, blind terror and ran and ran and ran and ran, down streets, around corners, across intersections, ignoring traffic and pedestrians ... and then she saw a couple of New York City blue-and-white police cruisers parked outside the Fifth Precinct. . .

June 1982

It doesn't take long to murder a child, and there are lots of ways to do it. You can shoot them, O.D. them, stab and strangle them, push them out of windows and off roofs, run them over with cars. A lot of my kids have died that way. More surely will.

There's another kind of death my kids experience, that leaves them, for a while, still breathing in and out, but inside their heads where they live, a corpse.

Three months on the street is a very long time. Six months is forever. A year? Then they're just breathing in and out but dead inside. The poison works quickly. The girls' faces show it first. The boys can hide it a little longer.

In the beginning the kids can still argue with me: Hey Bruce, he's no pimp — he's my boyfriend and he needs me. Hey Bruce, I can stop when I want. Hey Bruce, I'm just trying to make a few bucks. In the beginning they can still make distinctions between what they are inside their heads and what they do with their bodies. But after 100 or 500 or 1,000 johns it becomes difficult, and then impossible, to separate what you are from what you do. You become what you do. And you no longer care.

Somewhere along the process a child dies. He's been murdered. Each john has struck a blow. Each john teaches a kid 20 bucks' worth of what street life is all about. The code is very simple: intimidate or be intimidated, seduce or be seduced, get over on or be gotten over on, do it to somebody else first — and make sure you get paid. Don't believe anybody.

For my kids, every simple human gesture becomes suspect: An offer of a cup of coffee becomes the beginning of a seduction. "Look Bruce, it works this way. I see this john cruising 42nd Street, like say near the arcade where all the kids hang out. He stops to look in a camera store near the corner. I stop too. You gotta cigarette, mister? (That means I'm available, Bruce.) If he gives it to me, the contact is made. We just have to work out the details. . ."

God talk becomes extremely precarious, even risky. Let me tell you about "Our Father," Scott. Never mind that you never knew your own father, that he was never there for you. Our Father in heaven is different. He's always there. He sees you and knows you and loves you. You've just never met Him . . .

The boy looked me right in the eye. He spoke quietly and courteously: "I'm too busy right now, Bruce. No offense, okay, but I've got to make a few bucks. Your God is okay, I guess, but He's sure not part of anything I've been into. I sure hope He can't see what I'm going to have to do tonight. I do *have* to, Bruce. I don't like it very much, but I'm afraid to hate it too much.

"Thanks for running Under 21, Bruce, but I can't stay. I guess I don't like the street very much, but it's where I live. You've got some rules here, Bruce, and I can't take the curfew. Besides, there's something going on outside and I'm missing it. Tell you what, Bruce. I'll just go out for a while. It's only 2 a.m. and I'll just walk around the block a couple of times. See you later."

The kid paused a moment, his hand on the door knob, the door pushed open a few inches to let in the street noise. Outside a fire truck from the 38th Street firehouse hurtled by. Its deep, bellowing klaxon drowned out his words, but I could still see his lips moving. He waited until the truck had passed. . . "Your God has too many rules, Bruce," he said, "and I'd rather have you for my father."

He never came back. I knew he never would. I keep wondering and thinking that maybe if I were better, or smarter, or holier, or worked harder, or prayed more, I wouldn't lose so many.

1982 — 1984

BEN-AMI

"I Hoped You Wouldn't Hurt Me"

"How much do you go for?" I said.
"$80," he said, "but I do everything for that.
I can go for less."

    The innkeeper said, "No. I can't help you. Go away," he said.

    It was late at night. The inn was very crowded. The young couple was poor. The husband, frantic with anxiety, insisted and pleaded and argued desperately: "Look, my wife is going to have a baby any minute. Please, you've got to let us in." Clearly, there were no large tips forthcoming to inspire the innkeeper's compassion and understanding. You can't take responsibilty for every pilgrim and traveler and wanderer who knocks on your door, even if the girl is young and tired and about to have a baby.

    After he turned them away, I wonder if the innkeeper ever gave the young mother and her husband a second thought? Listen, I know exactly how that innkeeper felt. Maybe he'd had a bad day. He wasn't such a bad guy. You just can't assume he was an unfeeling, heartless wretch and sweep him out of your mind like so much dirt. He must have had his reasons. And besides, it turned out okay. The

*young couple found a cave on a hillside where some
shepherds stabled their animals. The 14-year-old
girl had her baby there. It turned out all right.*

*Two kids knocked on my door one night. It was
late and I had had a bad day. I didn't want to wake
up. I didn't want to answer the door. I was tired and
had gone to bed angry. A bunch of kids were bedded
down on the living room floor, and the six bunk beds
were filled. I had been mugged earlier that day and
one of my kids stole the grocery money—and I didn't
like any of my kids very much. They didn't appreciate me and weren't very grateful . . . Playing the role
of noble martyr to the hilt, I opened the door.*

*Two kids stood there, uncertainly, obviously
reading the look on my face. One of the kids said,
"Are you Bruce?" and I said, yes. And he said, "Do
you take kids in?" and I said, yes. "Can we stay with
you?" he said. And I said, "No, because we have no
room." The kid began to cry. "Where can we go?
What can I do?" he said. And I said, "You can go
back out into the street, and you can look sad."*

*The kid stopped crying, and he looked at me. "I
can do that," he said. So he did, or they did. They
both went back out into the street. One boy was 15,
the other was 14. I never saw them again.*

*I can still see their faces, just about as clearly
today as I could that night. I can still see the tears on
the boy's face. I can see how the other kid stood, and
the way he looked at me.*

*I wonder if the innkeeper kept remembering,
too.*

August 1983

The sun came out of the sea off Fort Lauderdale beach and I watched it make a morning begin.

I wasn't exactly crying. It's just that I couldn't stop the tears that kept forming in the corner of my eyes. I couldn't seem to hold them back. Every couple of minutes one would slip loose and start its quick run down my cheeks. I would catch it before it got too far. Nobody was there to see it, but I was still embarrassed.

I had gotten back to my room in the Sand Castle Motel at 4:30 a.m. I was really tired after a long day that began early in the morning in Houston.

The Sand Castle is the motel we would like to purchase for an Under 21 center in Fort Lauderdale, the runaway capital of the United States. Literally thousands of kids come there, hang out, and become part of a street scene that is as bad as any in the country. Many never make it back.

The Sand Castle is a block off the beach and an ideal location for a Covenant House.

It had been a very full day. I had flown direct from our brand new Houston center to yet another public meeting and series of interviews in Fort Lauderdale. Afterwards, I came back to the Sand Castle in my dark blue Hertz Mustang. It was about midnight. A Tuesday.

I guess I was too keyed up to sleep, so I decided to check out the Strip — that stretch of beach in Lauderdale beginning around Las Olas on the south to Sunset Boulevard on the north. During spring break, hundreds of thousands of college kids inundate the Strip in Fort Lauderdale. They bring millions of dollars to spend. The beach scene — portrayed in the July issue of *Playboy* — gets pretty wild. Hotels and motels make a lot of money off them. The Holiday Inn on the Strip leases to a bar that sponsors wet T-shirt contests and banana-eating contests. It's definitely not clean, wholesome, family fun.

Over the years, the Strip has developed a national reputation as a "fun" spot for kids. So if you've got to be a runaway and you're cold and hungry and homeless up north, you can always choose to be just hungry and homeless. Anything goes on the Strip. And at least you're not cold anymore. And you can make money.

My blue Mustang was instantly anonymous. So was its balding, fiftyish driver in slacks and T-shirt. Just another john cruising. . .

From midnight to 4:30 a.m. I cruised the Strip — south down to Las Olas, cutting over to Birch Road, driving north to the Sand Castle and then back down A1A, crisscrossing on each side street, running every block, east to west, inward and then back out to the ocean.

It was a quiet night, but there were still dozens of kids working. Some would just stand provocatively — the hustler's stance. Others would make those minute, secret hand signals. The bolder ones just beckoned or whistled or called. My stopping for red lights gave still other striplings the opportunity to wander over and wonder if I was looking for some action. No thanks, I said.

It was getting on toward 3 a.m. and I was pretty tired and had decided to pack it in. One more trip, I thought. The streets were rapidly emptying and the girls and the boy hustlers stood out now even more obviously.

Heading north, I stopped for a red light on Ocean Boulevard and looked out over the now-deserted beach. I didn't see the kid approach my car and was startled when he spoke to me.

"Do you want to give me a ride?" he said.

He was a nice-looking kid, 16, maybe 17, I thought. Nice eyes, nice hair. A little scared, maybe.

"Sure," I said. The kid opened the door and slid gracefully into the front seat. I took my foot off the brake and the Mustang moved slowly north up A1A. By now it knew the way.

"Are you a cop?" he said.

"No, I said," and laughed — mostly to put the kid at ease. "Do I look like a cop?" I said.

"You can never tell," he said.

"I guess not," I said. "I'm not. My name is Bruce," I said.

"My name is Dan," he said.

"Where're you from?" I said.

"Minnesota," he said."

"How long have you been in Fort Lauderdale?" I asked and turned off A1A on to Las Olas.

"Three weeks," he said.

"Where are you staying?" I said.

"In a motel," he said, "but I lost my room."

I drove south on Birch Road and made a decision to continue the conversation.

"How are you surviving?" I said. "How are you making it?"

"Hustling," he said.

"Are you hustling now?" I said.

"Yes," he said.

"How much do you go for?" I said.

"$80," he said, and hastily added, "but I do everything for that. I can go for less," he said.

And then my eyes began to burn and then they began to glisten and blurred oncoming headlights and I was glad it was dark in the car and he couldn't see the tears forming.

"How old are you?" I asked. It was getting hard for me to talk.

"Eighteen," he said, although there was not much conviction in his voice, as though he didn't really expect me to believe him. (I didn't.) He was a nice-looking kid. A gentle face. "How long have you been hustling?" I said.

"I ran away to L.A. when I was 15 and got into it there," he said. "I've moved around a lot," he said.

The blue Mustang seemed to drive itself up Birch Road, and I pulled it over on a quiet side street a couple of blocks from where the kid jumped into my car.

I turned to face the kid, and I guess he could see the tears in my eyes. He looked at me a little uncertainly.

"Hey," I said, "I enjoyed riding with you.

Thanks," I said. I reached into my pocket for a $20 bill. "This will help you with your motel room," I said. The kid became very still, his eyes frozen for a moment on nothing I could see.

"This is certainly different," he said.

"I know," I said. "Be good to yourself," I said. "Take care of yourself," I said. The kid hesitated — he didn't want to get out of the car. He opened his mouth to speak and then changed his mind.

I touched him on the shoulder. "Be good to yourself," I said again.

"Thanks," he said. "I hoped you wouldn't hurt me," he said.

The boy got out of the car. "Thanks," he said. "Later," he said.

"Later," I said. I drove back to the Sand Castle. It was almost 4:30 a.m. I was really tired.

I wasn't crying exactly. I just couldn't stop the tears, so I decided to watch the sun come up.

"I hoped you wouldn't hurt me," he said.

To See the Elephant

*"I missed not coming here for a long time.
I never see my kids enough."*

January 1984

I saw an innocent kid today. His face wasn't but I think he was. There was too much pain and longing in his eyes for him, at least at that moment, not to have been innocent.

It got me thinking: Did I want to be innocent again? I'm not really sure. Could I even stand it? What would happen to all my hard and painfully won knowledge — about myself, my kids, the world in general, the healthy ingrained suspicion of my motives? If I became innocent again? Would I lose it all? Would I have to go through it all over again?

This kid had definitely been around the horn. I mean, to use an earlier metaphor, he had definitely "seen the elephant" — and had been trampled . . . He wouldn't take his eyes off me but I didn't mind. I mean, I wasn't uncomfortable. Even though he was crying.

I was in one of our centers after being away too long, for a visit, a board of directors and an all-staff meeting — and also, to celebrate a pre-Christmas Mass for our staff and kids.

I was surprised at how many kids came to the Mass. I didn't expect so many. Almost 50. I was surprised at how attentive they were (and how well they sang).

I watched the kid watching me and decided to throw out my prepared sermon— it was directed more to an adult audience, and I knew the kids would not "hear" it. I knew *he* wouldn't.

"Hey," I said, to all the kids, to everybody, but really, only to him. "I'm really glad you're here. I hope you stay around. I missed not coming here for a long time. I never see my kids enough.

"Most people don't know this," I said, "but most of the really important things I've learned about myself, I learned from you. It took me a while to understand that," I said.

This kid wouldn't take his eyes off me. His face got stiller and stiller, his eyes more watchful. He was skinny and 17.

"In the beginning," I said, "when you kids were crowding into my apartment, I listened to your needs. That's all I could really hear then. It took me a long time to learn to listen to *you*. That's when I began to learn about myself," I said.

"That's when I began to understand how good you are and how brave you are and what a gift God gave me when he gave me you. Thank you," I said, "for being here so we can love you. (I wanted to say "*I* love you," but I chickened out in mid-sentence.)

"That's what Christmas is all about," I said. "That's why God came as Jesus. So we can love God the way I love you. So we can touch him the way I touch you.

"Thank you for changing me," I said. "More than anyone else, when I needed changing, you did it. Thank you for making me grow," I said. "It was really painful and I didn't want to, but I did. You really changed my life," I said. "I owe you. I really care a lot about you," I said.

It wasn't a sermon really. I just wanted to thank the kids for being my Christmas present.

After Mass was over I moved around to meet the kids. It was really great. I loved being there. It was no accident that we met in the middle of a crowd of kids, but nobody else was there.

"Where are you from?" I said.

"It doesn't matter," he said. "I just came back. I've been here before," he said, "but I've got a drinking problem. . ." "I can see it in your face," I said.

"I've tried really hard," he said. "I'm afraid," he said. He was a skinny 17-year-old kid with a shop-worn face and haunted eyes and a batttered smashed-out-flat ego. There were no barriers between us. The pain was there, and the fear. He wanted to give them to me but there was no way I could take them. Our pain is our pain.

The innocence was there, too. I think if you hurt enough and are afraid enough and alone enough, the pain, for a time, pushes back the bad and corrupt part of us, the evil habits, and lets the innocence show through. Maybe pain creates innocence. Maybe pain pushes us back through all the garbage and dirt to the time when we were clean. When we were children. And innocent.

Unless you become as little children you shall not enter the Kingdom of Heaven. Did Jesus mean that? Did Jesus mean that our good and evil are measured by love and pain? And that becoming innocent again means reliving the pain? I understood better then what purgatory must be like. And I was very afraid.

"Look," I said. "You've got to get it together."

"I know," he said.

"Stay with it, " I said. "Let us help you," I said. "Don't go away," I said. "Stay around," I said. "I'm glad you're here," I said.

"I know," he said. And he smiled an innocent smile. And for just a moment the pain was gone from his eyes and I understood that innocence destroys the pain that restored it.

"See you around," I said.

"Later," he said.

"What's your name?" I said.

"Michael," he said.

Lent 1984

"You were always like a father to me," he said. He was just one of the 30 or more overflow kids we had bedded down on the floor that night.

I didn't know his name. I didn't remember his face.

"Thanks," I said. "I'm glad I was," I said. It was 6:45 a.m. on Ash Wednesday.

I had just come downstairs from my room on the fifth floor and was passing through the ground floor of our center on my way to morning prayer in our Community Chapel.

"You really were," he said.

"Thanks," I said.

Another kid noticed my prayer book under my arm. "You've got your Bible," he announced.

"Yes," I said. "Morning prayer begins at 7 a.m."

"You wouldn't catch me praying at 7 a.m.," another kid said.

He was one of half a dozen kids standing around in their jockey shorts waiting to iron their pants.

This was a pretty tough bunch of kids. The older ones. The ones who have been on the street too long. The used-up ones. Most don't really expect to make it: their short, final journey already begun.

Every night, when the kids are sleeping, our staff gathers their meager belongings — the inevitable pair of jeans and a shirt — and takes the soiled clothing downstairs to our laundry. When the kids wake up they can put on clean clothes. It's really important that they dress clean.

Every day half a dozen kids insist on lining up to iron their only pair of pants. They wait patiently, standing around in their jockey shorts, or with a towel wrapped around their waist, for their turn at the ironing board.

They want to look good, even if they do have

only one pair of pants.

They have a hard time understanding why they are not going to make it, and why their dying has to be so hard.

A street kid? The used-up ones? With one pair of pants? I wonder if they are maybe closer to You than I am? I mean there's their aloneness and fear and terror and abandonment...They shared that with You. I never did.

A street kid hoping for a father who won't forget his name and face, who doesn't know how to say prayers but wants to look good in his only pair of pants...

Do You love him more than You love me?

I guess if I were you, God, I would.

Easter 1984

It was 14 years ago when I met this 9-year-old kid. That September Sunday morning he was sitting three rows back from the pulpit in a small mountain parish in upstate New York, safely scrunched in between his five sisters — and all of them carefully bookended by a vigilant father and mother.

I was there for the weekend, preaching at all the Masses — nine times — trying to raise money to take care of my kids back in New York. His name was Billy.

His mouth was halfway open and he was listening hard. Some of the things I had to say weren't easy to hear.

Covenant House was just a half dozen ramshackle roach-and-rat-infested apartments on the Lower East Side then, about 30 randy street kids living with this perpetually tired priest.

I had more hair then, and my voice hadn't yet darkened to its present soft rasp.

I was broke, as usual, and couldn't pay the rent, and as usual, couldn't afford the food, couldn't buy the clothes my kids needed. And so I begged.

The mountains framing the little church were absolutely beautiful. An early fall had splashed the ravines and hillsides with color, and the air was crisp and clean. I spoke of my own hot, dirty streets and my own beautiful kids and how good they were.

This little kid never stopped listening. He closed his mouth every now and then to swallow.

I got to know him and his family very well over the years, returning often as to a second home to that village in the mountains and that beautiful family.

I'm going to come down and help you some day, Billy would say to me. When I'm old enough, he said. When my mom and dad will let me, he said. When I finish school, he said. When I finish college, he said. Year after year he said it. Because I loved him very much I wanted to believe him.

In his last year of college he wrote, "I'm coming. Tell me when." I loved him too much to say don't come, so I didn't answer his letter.

He came anyway, to join our faith community — the exactly 100 volunteers: teachers, doctors, lawyers, a journalist, retired businessmen, grandmothers, engineers, nurses, recent college graduates, a farmer, — who live with me on Eighth Avenue (or in one of our other centers) and help me, full-time, with our kids.

They each promise to commit at least a full year to God and my kids.

In exchange I provide room and board and $10 a week ($12, if they insist; salary is negotiable up to $12 a week). I also provide an opportunity to practice the corporal and spiritual works of mercy: to feed the hungry, to clothe the naked, to shelter the homeless, to comfort my kids.

I ask them to pray together three hours a day and to fast once a week.

I am inordinately proud of them, and I love them very much.

They are the Resurrection happening all over again. Christ alive in them, living through them. Causing grace and goodness and love and life to occur once more in the murdered lives of our kids at Covenant House.

How else can the Resurrection occur in the life of a dying child? If not through love?

"It must have been that God led me down here," said Billy. "I couldn't seem not to come."

He starts tomorrow, working on our third floor, the one we reserve for the hundreds and hundreds of desperate young teenage mothers who will come to us this year. Who will walk in off the streets with their week-and month-old babies they didn't want to abort. They had no place to live, and you can't raise a brand new baby in a phone booth or a doorway of an abandoned building.

In this enormous country, filled with compassionate people, the wealthiest country in the world, that just shouldn't happen to a brand new baby.

Billy is a lover. It pours out of him. He would burst wide open if he tried to contain it.

Billy will be a resurrection for these kids with their babies. He will be Easter for them.

He is an Easter for me.

It's almost 15 years since I saw him in that little mountain church. I had 30 kids then and knew and loved them all, and I was their Easter.

More than 15,000 kids will come to Covenant House this year.

I need more Billys. To be resurrections. Please, come.

Write first. *You've got to write first.* Mark the envelope "Faith Community" so it gets right to my desk.

1984 — 1987

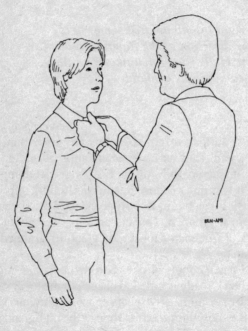

"I Ain't a Bad Kid. . ."

*His right thumb pointed somewhere
in the direction of the Pacific Ocean,
in the Hollywood hitchhiker's gesture.
It meant he was available.*

September 1984

"You'll have goose bumps on goose bumps," my friend said as he handed me a ticket for the opening ceremonies of the Los Angeles Olympics.

It was one of those once-in-a-lifetime opportunities. I was out in Los Angeles anyway, speaking before a group of Franciscan superiors about the work of Covenant House, so I gleefully grabbed the ticket.

I had a couple of days before the games began, and had already decided to check out the local street scene once more. Five years ago, on a previous visit, I was exposed for the first time to the malignant evil in the City of Angels that corrupts and destroys thousands of homeless kids on the streets of Hollywood.

It was no better now. Maybe even worse. I drove up and down Santa Monica Boulevard — the most notorious meat rack in the country — half a dozen times. It was as I had remembered it. I could have picked up at least 50 kids. They seemed younger, more hopeless than before.

I stopped for a red light on the corner of LaBrea and Santa Monica. A kid was sprawled on a bench there, facing the oncoming traffic. His left leg was thrown casually over the back of the bench, the other stretched straight out along the seat. His right thumb pointed somewhere in the direction of the Pacific Ocean, in the Hollywood hitchhiker's gesture. It meant he was available.

He seemed to be about 16. An average, everyday kind of kid. A nice kid.

The light took a long time. We looked at each other. I didn't say anything. He didn't either.

The light turned green and I took my foot off the brake and my eyes off the boy.

"I ain't a bad kid," he said suddenly, softly.

The car was already moving, and I was afraid to look back — the traffic was very heavy. I didn't stop. There was not much I could have said to him. At that time of night — it was about one in the morning — there was no place I could have taken him.

I wondered what he saw in my face. Did he see the dismay and sadness and misunderstand? Did he think I was condemning him for trying to pick me up? Or maybe, something else? Did he see concern? Did he suspect that I cared? Did he know that I liked him?

I thought about driving around the block and

trying to talk to the kid, but I didn't.

Los Angeles has thousands of kids like that. I mean thousands. There is really no place for them to go where they can get the kind of very special help they need. (According to a recent article in *USA TODAY*, there are only 50 beds available in the entire area, and most of these are not set up to help girls and boys like these.)

Dionne Warwick sang a song about Hollywood and lost kids like that: "All the stars that never were, are parking cars and pumping gas." And displaying their wares on the Santa Monica meat rack.

I went to bed that night depressed, sad and angry.

My dark mood was quickly dispelled the next day, Saturday. The weather for the opening ceremonies was flawless. Anxious to avoid the expected traffic jams, I arrived early at the Los Angeles Coliseum. For the next hour I watched enthralled as tens of thousands of people quickly filled the almost 100,000 seats.

I couldn't get that kid out of my mind! Despite the magnificent pageantry. I wished, too late, that I had stopped and at least talked to him. I wished I hadn't blown the chance to tell him I thought he was a good kid.

The final event, the Parade of the Athletes, was absolutely inspiring as the best and finest, the most disciplined and superbly conditioned and gifted young people in the world marched into the stadium. The welcoming ovation for the American athletes was mind blowing: "USA, USA, USA"— the chant was thunderous.

I had this big lump in my throat. I mean, here I am, almost 58 — I've been around the horn a few times — and I had this big patriotic red, white and blue lump in my throat!

I will never forget those three glorious hours in the L.A. Coliseum. The best and finest young people in the world, from every nation in the world. And just a few miles away, a young kid hanging out on a street corner bench. . .

I don't think I will ever forget the face of that kid. It's tucked away in an unquiet corner of my mind that I reserve for sad, unfinished memories.

I wish I could have helped him. No, that's a copout. I wish I did help him. I hope he knew I thought he was a good kid. I hope that's what he saw in my face.

I would really love the opportunity to open a Covenant House for kids like him in Los Angeles.

October 1984

I had seen this kid around the center a few times. We had nodded at each other, said hello. He was easy to remember. Dark, quiet eyes, quiet face — no longer a boy's face. Too watchful. Too careful.

Each time we had passed in the corridors or in the lounge, he would look at me intently, longer than necessary, as though he wanted me to know something about him. Or maybe, it was the other way around.

I saw him again — the second time that day —

outside our center where a documentary was being filmed about street kids and Covenant House.

"I'm Rick," he said. "I volunteered to be one of the technical consultants for the documentary."

"Oh?" I said.

"Yeah," he said. "The director didn't really know how the street works, or how the kids really are."

"Not many people do," I said.

"*I* do," he said.

"You've been around?" I said. It was more a statement of fact than a question, but he answered anyway.

"I've been in San Francisco and Los Angeles and New Orleans and Fort Lauderdale. In Houston, too. I looked for you when I was in L.A.," he said, "but you weren't there."

"I know," I said. "We don't have a Covenant House there."

"So then I ended up at your center," he said.

"I'm glad you did," I said. "I'm really glad you're here."

"Thanks," he said. "Thanks for starting Covenant House."

"Thank *God*," I said.

"No," he said. "Thank *you*."

"Don't you believe in God?" I said.

Rick shrugged slightly. "Why should I?" he said. "God *never* did anything for me." He paused for a moment and gave me another one of those curious, intent looks. "It's been pretty bad for me,

Bruce. I'm a drifter— four years." (He spaced out the words slowly with a quiet exactitude that tore my heart.) "Have been since I was 14. There's not much about me that you would want to know. God either." He gave a grim little hurting smile.

"You're *here*," I said "and that's enough," I said. "We don't have to start anywhere else. I think God sent you here."

"No he didn't," Rick said. "I needed a place to stay. That's all. A john dropped me off. Not God. Why should God care about what happens to me? Why should I care about God?"

"Did you ever fall in love with somebody?" I said. "Really in love?"

He nodded slightly.

"Did they ever ask you why you loved them? Did you have a reason? Did you need a reason?"

"No," he said.

"Neither does God," I said. "He doesn't need to have you love him back."

"That's good," he said, "because I don't."

"Your big scene is coming up, Bruce. You know, the one where you talk about those six kids who knocked on your door after they made the porno film. The ones that started Covenant House."

"I'm no actor," I said. "I hate this part of it. How can I act the part of being me? Besides, the director wants me to look old and haggard and worn out after worrying about my kids for 16 years. I'd rather look young and skinny and handsome," I said.

"Like Robert Redford?" he said. And we

grinned at each other.

"You'll do just great," he said. And then he gave me a rib-crunching hug. I hugged him back.

"Thanks," he said.

"Thank God," I said.

"No," he said, "thank you."

"Maybe thank God?" I said.

"Maybe," he said. It's easier to trust you, Bruce. You're here. I never saw God and I never will."

"Don't be so sure," I said. "You will," I said. "If *I* will you will," I said.

At the end, the reporter asked me why I do what I do. "I do what I do because of God," I answered. "And sometimes, God has a kid's face."

It wasn't hard to play that scene. I just kept thinking of God and seeing Rick's face.

"I'll Never Let You Be My Friend. . ."

He was very emphatic about it.
Trusting people was not Tony's style.

June 1985

"If you're going to make it, Tony, you'll need a mentor. I'd like to be that for you," I said.

"What's a mentor, Bruce?" The kid in my office twisted uneasily in his chair, crossing and uncrossing his Adidas. He had big hands and feet — the rest of him hadn't caught up yet. His eyes were very dark and very guarded.

"It's like being a teacher, Tony," I said, "but like being more of a friend than a teacher, an adult friend."

"I'll never let you be my friend, Bruce," the boy said quickly. "You can be my father or mother, you can be my brother, my uncle but never my friend. You get over on friends, Bruce — you con them."

He was very emphatic about it. Trusting people was not Tony's style. Not much happens on the street that makes you want to trust anybody. You just get hurt that way; people will get over every time. Friends are just dudes on the street who haven't hurt you yet.

The kid had a lot of fire in him. I liked that. It's the quiet, passive ones, the kids who have already given up, who are the most difficult to reach. The street squeezes all the juice out of a kid. The best way to handle the pain, the despair, the knowing how it's all going to end, is not to care anymore, not to let it get to you.

The "best" way to handle the street is with a bottle of beer or cheap wine in your hand and a pocketful of ludes or big reds. The "best" way to handle the loneliness and the fear is some grass with some friends.

So they get over on you. You get over on them. Nobody trusts nobody. . .

The kids with the fire still in them, the kids still capable of passion and caring, the kids still capable of anger and hate — these are the ones who can make it back if you can turn the anger and hate around, back into positive energy.

Without a mentor, somebody who can kick around inside a kid's head, talk to him about his attitudes, about why he does what he does, about how important it is to meet other people halfway. . .a kid won't make it.

(Only God can help the bummed-out, used-up kids. And, after a year on the street there aren't any other kind. What He usually does is help them die.)

How can you teach a kid to trust again, to take a chance on another person, to believe in another person? Especially when he can't trust himself or believe in himself anymore?

You love him. And if you really do that, and if you don't stop — and you survive his testing, and if you do love him — then a kid can begin to believe that he really is okay, really good, really worth it, because nobody would love a piece of garbage.

"Tony," I said, "I can't be your father or mother. I don't want to be your sister or brother or uncle. I want to be your friend and I won't get over on you. Trust me," I said. "At least begin to believe that you at least want to," I said.

"Let me teach you about passion," I said, "and about compromise. Let me teach you about good anger and good hate and how to conform," I said.

"I don't know what you're talking about," he said.

"I know," I said. "But you really do. It's just that you haven't put the words together in your head yet. That's what a mentor is for," I said. "And to be a friend."

"Why is it so important for you to be my friend?" he said.

"Because I can't be anything else," I said. "If I can't be your friend, I can't be anybody whom you can care about."

"Oh," he said. "I understand," he said. "I understand," he said. He smiled at me and relaxed totally, slouching down so far in his chair that he hung his head on the back of it.

"That's lesson number one in trust," I said.

"I know," he said.

I didn't talk to Tony about God. Tony is not ready for God yet. A mentor has to be up close and personal. God's not there yet. God can be his mentor after I get Tony ready.

The High Priestess
of Hedonism

*The high priestess of hedonism
has blessed premarital sex
— and just about every other kind.*

October 1985

Driving back into New York City from Newark Airport late last Sunday, I punched on my car radio, pushing randomly at the buttons. I was looking for a few soothing ballads to while away the end of a long day.

What I got was FM 97 WYNY and Dr. Ruth Westheimer holding forth on her weekly NBC radio show, Sexually Speaking. The high-pitched nervous laugh was instantly recognizable.

I listened in fascinated horror while she delightedly praised Pete, a 17-year-old boy, because he could bring his girlfriend to multiple orgasms.

"You're so lucky to have such a girlfriend," she chortled to this 17-year-old kid. (He had a nice clean-cut voice.) "Don't share her with anybody," she advised.

Pete was overjoyed. (His voice had an appealing golly-gee-whiz quality.) "You're really great, Dr.

Ruth, but I need some more advice," the young voice said. "I think I have multiple orgasms too, when my girlfriend performs oral sex on me," he said. "Is that possible?"

Dr. Ruth's voice positively beamed with pleasure. I mean, she was ecstatic. "Of course," she said, but added a cautionary note. "As you get older you won't be able to have as many orgasms as you do now!"

In her final benediction to this young Lothario, Dr. Ruth urged him to wear a T-shirt saying, "I'm the greatest lover in Washington, D.C."

Now, maybe you think I should have turned off Dr. Ruth, splashed some holy water on the car radio, and pulled out my rosary. I did no such thing. I listened unbelievingly through a short station break to find out what she would say to the next caller.

He turned out to be — his description— a respected, happily married man of some prominence in the community. He loved his wife. She loved him. They had nice kids.

There was only one small problem: His wife wanted him to watch her having sex with another woman. It would liven up their marriage.

Dr. Ruth was wary. Dr. Ruth felt that he might be sexually attracted to this other woman and that the green-eyed monster of jealousy could wreck the marriage!

Dr. Ruth hit on the perfect solution immediately. "Why don't you go down to your friendly neighborhood video store," she said, "and rent a porno film of two women making love. You could both watch it together. Maybe that will satisfy her fantasy."

The respected, happily married man of some prominence coughed apologetically. "I think that's the problem," he said. "We've already done that. I think that's where she got the idea," he said.

What are we to think of the enormously popular— and influential — Dr. Ruth? Leave her to heaven? Laugh at her?

What are we to think of NBC radio that brings this insane drivel to tens of millions of homes every week?

What, more importantly, are we to think about ourselves and the part we all play in the creation of our totally eroticized society?

And, most of all, what are we going to say to that 17-year-old boy and his teenage girlfriend and their millions of brothers and sisters in the United States? Dr. Ruth has just given them all permission to have practically unlimited sex anytime they want, as long as they're "protected" of course. That means it's perfectly okay as long as they use contraceptives!

The high priestess of hedonism has blessed premarital sex — and just about every other kind.

Maybe the real question for all of us is: What have we already taught our kids about the beauty and goodness of sex within a wholesome, loving marriage? That can help them put into perspective the nonsense taught by Dr. Ruth?

Maybe the real question is: When did we teach them? Did we ever teach them?

Or did we leave that sacred duty of education in responsible sexuality to the Dr. Ruths of this world? And to the purveyors of the hard-core pornography that has become a cultural universal in our society and that has become the chief source of information on sex for our children.

We cannot hide any longer from the bitter truth that our kids are turning to the Dr. Ruths for the information about sex that we have denied them — or, at the very least, have made little effort to provide.

Not everything that Dr. Ruth says is errant nonsense. She deals explicitly, directly and simply with a great deal of factual material about human sexuality that our young people — and old people, too — find informative and interesting.

It is Dr. Ruth's almost totally secular and incredibly hedonistic value system that offends and distresses — and tragically misleads—millions of people who see human sexuality as sacred and wholesome.

For men and women of faith, however, fidelity, sacrifice, commitment, and dignity nurture the almost divine creativity found in the fullness of love between a man and a woman. And, more importantly, safeguard the strong, wholesome families that are the bedrock of any society that hopes to survive.

Look, the more our families and our society are flooded with the kinds of intellectual and moral garbage now poisoning our social environment, the more our kids need age-appropriate, value-laden education in affective sexuality.

And, if we do not personally feel up to the task of providing this education ourselves, we must insist that our schools — both public and private— take the obligation seriously.

I am not naive about the difficulty involved. We live in a religiously pluralistic society. We must all work together to provide the basic common teaching materials that will illuminate instead of distort the beauty and intimacy of human sexuality.

It will not be easy, but it can be done because it must be done. Until we do, Dr. Ruth will happily fill in for us.

That 17-year-old kid — the one with the nice clean-cut, golly-gee-whiz voice — might be your kid or my kid. He has a right to be protected from the high priests and priestesses of sexual license who make millions of dollars celebrating lust while they warp the attitudes and morals of our children.

Christmas 1985

Merry Christmas, mister. Hey mister, do you wanna party? Are you looking for a good time. . .on Christmas Eve?

It's 10 bucks for the Globe Hotel and 20 bucks for me, mister. . . Give yourself a Christmas present, mister.

Jeez, I've got to stop crying. Nobody is going to buy me if I'm crying. It's bad for the john's head. It wrecks his fantasy when a kid he wants to buy has tears in her eyes.

I feel like such a jerk. Working the Cameo on Christmas Eve. People look at me real quick and then look away. Except the johns.

Bruce wants me to come to church on Christmas. He says God won't mind at all. In fact, He'd like to see me there, Bruce says.

I'd be afraid. With these clothes on! Midnight Mass would never be the same! Besides, if I ever tried to sing "Silent Night" I'd start to cry. Can you imagine me in church singing "Silent Night?" God would laugh.

Before He got mad, God would laugh.

I wish I could call my mother. It would be nice to know if she's okay. It being Christmas and all. She'd want to know what I was doing and where, but she already knows, and it would spoil her Christmas to know I was alive.

I wonder if she'd rather think I was dead. Maybe it wouldn't hurt her so much then. She could go back to thinking how it used to be on Christmas. When I was little. Before I left. Before I ruined things. Before Dad died. . .

Jeez, I've got to stop crying. Blue Fly will get real mad if he sees me crying.

Bruce says I should come to Covenant House for Christmas. The place looks great, he says. Christmas trees and presents for the kids and a big turkey dinner.

It's hard when it's somebody else's Christmas tree. You walk around all day long thinking of the time when you had one all your own.

When you had a family, and you got presents, and you were with people who loved you and who wanted to have you around.

It's hard to get presents from somebody you barely know. Who you never saw before yesterday. Who are just trying to make you feel good and be happy.

Sometimes it just makes it worse. It's Christmas and everybody wants me to be happy.

Except Blue Fly! He wants me to work the Cameo porno theater and pick up l0 johns. Maybe they'll be sorry for me and give me some big tips — before they go home to their own wives and kids and decorate their own Christmas trees!

I wonder what kind of presents they're going to give the kids at Covenant House this year. I wonder if they'd let me in again, one more time. Bruce says he will.

My pimp, Blue Fly, sure won't like it. He really hassled me the last time I went to Covenant House. He beat me real bad. I don't want to go through that again!

I sure don't want to keep doing this either.

Maybe Bruce is right and God won't get mad at me on Christmas.

Kids Like You
Don't Have Funerals

"There's no other place I can go, Bruce,
where I want to go.
Where they want me to come."

"Bruce, I've been here 24 times! Since I was 14, Bruce. I'm 20 now. I'm really scared to turn 21. I won't be able to come back anymore, when I'm 21.

"Covenant House is my home, Bruce. I don't have anybody else," Timmy said. "What do I do, Bruce?"

The issue between us was a deadly serious one. For Timmy and for me. And for Covenant House and for thousands of other kids like Timmy.

You see, 16,000 different kids will come into Covenant House residences around the country this year. About 4,000 of them are repeaters — we've seen them before.

Of that 4,000, about half return two or three times before they make it. Or before they don't.

The others, like Timmy, are constant visitors. Unable to make it at Covenant House, unable to make it on their own, or on the street, they move in and out of our program or other shelters around the country.

There are easily tens of thousands of these kids in the United States. They are America's street kids.

Timmy has the record at Covenant House for returning. Twenty-four times he has come back to us! (Timmy knows the rules better than half our staff.)

What do you do with the Timmys? The repeater kids?

I sighed for the thousandth time, as I pondered that question once more. Are we helping these kids at all, by being good to them? Are we, maybe, making them dependent on us?

Should we be more hard-nosed and put a limit on the number of times a kid can come back? For the sake of the other kids? For the sake of our staff? To save money? To make more beds readily available for kids we can help?

Please God, can I — should I — write off the Timmys and leave them to Your mercy?

As professionals, we know they're not going to make it. We all know that. Including the kids. Everybody knows that they are permanently disconnected from society.

Can I, should I, disconnect them from Covenant House after, say five or maybe even 10 tries here?

Can I pull the plug . . . ? Should I? As a humane, caring professional, musn't I? For the sake of the other kids. . . ?

I sighed again and looked at Timmy, and decided that one of his most irresistable qualities was that slow, sad smile on an incongruously cheerful face. I have a weakness for lost skinny kids with sad smiles.

Timmy's six-inch-thick file lay on my desk. In clinical, detached, professional language it spelled out the biography of an American street kid:

When, at age 14, he couldn't take the beatings and the fights and the not being wanted anymore, Timmy ran away. Our case records methodically list the bruises and scars on his body.

At age 14, on the run, nothing or nobody at Covenant House could hold him down. Foster homes didn't do it either. Or hospitals.

Timmy was a nice kid. I mean really nice, when we first met him six years ago. He just couldn't connect with anybody long enough to take a chance and settle down to loving someone, or letting someone love him.

He drifted in and out of dozens of programs and cities and relationships, always coming back to us. Glad to see us. Glad to be back home for a few days. For a couple of weeks. For a whole month!

Timmy stopped being a runaway at 16. The law in New York says you can no longer be a runaway once you blow the candles out on your 16th birthday cake. The law says you're just a homeless kid who can't go home and can't get into foster care without a battle. You just have to make it any way you can.

At age 16 you've got problems you never dreamed about when you couldn't stand the beatings and the not being loved by anybody and ran to the street.

You didn't think about the fact that at age 16, without a high school diploma, you wouldn't be able to get a job.

You didn't know that at age 16 you couldn't legally register in a hotel.

You find out that welfare workers and Family Court officials will tell you to go back home, even though you can't.

You did know that the law says you're too young to drink or vote.

You didn't know that you had practically no rights at all.

You found out real quick at age 16 that to make it on the street you had to get into some pretty rotten things.

You found out that in New York State in the United States of America, at age 16 the law says you can legally make a porn film. Legally!

New York State says that you're too young and immature to drink, vote, find housing, work, get medical help — but that you're old enough to take off your clothes and stand in front of a camera and become a porn star. It's legal to do that, if you're cold and hungry and homeless and need money.

If you're lucky, before you have to do this stuff, you'll find out about Covenant House and our open door policy — that Covenant House is easy to get into 24 hours a day, no questions asked.

But 24 times! Twenty-four times in six years?

"Timmy," I said, "are we any good for you at all? Is our being good to you good for you?

"Isn't there any end to it?" I said. "Twenty-four times! That's a record, Timmy. That's the most times any kid has ever come back to Covenant House."

"I like it here, Bruce. I like the staff. They like it when I come back. They're glad to see me. There's no other place I can go, Bruce, where I want to go. Where they want me to come."

He didn't look desperate. He just looked sad. Even when he smiled.

There isn't anything really wrong with Timmy. He just doesn't know how to stay alive. Or what to do, or where to go, or what to say, or what to think about anything.

Twenty-four times our teams of professionals devised a treatment plan for Timmy: a foster home, a drug program, a good job training facility, medical and educational and psychological services, etc., etc., etc.

Twenty-four times we and he failed. That is, Timmy couldn't make it. He didn't make it.

We don't know what to do about Timmy and we love him.

I can't pull the plug on Timmy. I just can't. Even if I should, I won't. I don't care if that makes me unprofessional.

Timmy clutters up my life. I'm glad he does. I guess I'd rather have him around than out on the street knowing he couldn't come back.

I couldn't stand knowing that he knew that he couldn't come back. Besides, I'd miss him.

Until he turns 21. Then I won't let myself miss him anymore.

June 1986

I looked at the boy across my desk, trying to describe him to myself, but it was hard.

Average height, dark blond hair, dusky blue eyes. Bold eyes. Bright eyes. Brave, direct eyes.

"My name is Peter," he said.

Not exactly skinny, but not well muscled. Not exactly effeminate, but not strongly masculine either. Sexually indefinite, I thought. A young looking 16.

"My name is Bruce," I said.

He wore his low-slung jeans and green T-shirt with casually-studied nonchalance. The Etonic running shoes looked new. He had big feet.

"That apartment you were in today," I said, "is owned by a guy into sadomasochism, sex with kids your age, and a lot of drugs. He's got a 19-year-old lover who makes porn films with a felony warrant for assault out on him."

"I'm 16," Peter said. This piece of irrelevance hung in the air between us.

"I know about the guy," Peter said. "The cops told me about him. They wanted me to say that he gave me drugs and had sex with us. I didn't tell them anything."

"My kids tell me you did," I said.

"He treated me good, Bruce. He didn't hurt me. He's real rich. I want some of that, Bruce."

"You want the clothes and the nice apartments and the grass and the trips to the Bahamas, the nice restaurants. . . He promised you all that," I said. It wasn't a question.

"I can get it, Bruce. I want it. I never want to go home to Georgia. I won't go."

"I called your mother," I said. "She wants you to come home."

"My mother's okay, Bruce, but there's nothing for me in Georgia. I won't go back. I'm going to make it in New York. If the cops send me home I'll just come back to New York."

"This guy will sell you to his friends," I said. "He already has. My kids told me about it. They're worried about you. A kid heading for trouble is how Billy described you."

"I won't let them hurt me, Bruce. If they try I'll blackmail them. I already know a lot about them. I can hurt them."

"They'll kill you," I said. "Real quick if you try that. You'll fall out of a window. You'll overdose. You'll just disappear. The death certificate — if they find your body, and they don't very often — will just say some dumb kid OD'd or killed himself. There won't be anything to investigate. Kids like you don't have funerals."

The boy didn't turn away. He wasn't embarrassed or ashamed. His dark, blue eyes looked at me thoughtfully.

"I've thought about all that, Bruce." His voice was soft but definite. "I appreciate your worrying about me. It's nice of you to do that. The cop too," he said.

"I wasn't trying to scare you," I said. "Just not to scare you. But it's a real bad scene and most kids never really make it out."

Peter didn't take his eyes off me. He was kind and attentive and listened carefully.

"You're going to be worth too much money to them," I said. "You'll be income producing property worth tens of thousands of dollars. They won't let you go," I said. "Until it's too late to matter. They'll want you to take your clothes off for a camera and you won't be able to say no."

"I'm going to make it in New York, Bruce. I figure I can make it as a hustler. If I have to."

"What about AIDS?" I said. "Hustlers can't practice safe sex. It's a sure bet you'll get AIDS."

"I hope not, Bruce ," he said. "I worry about that. That's the kind of sex I like, Bruce."

"When did you know you were gay?" I said.

"When I was 12 or 13 I was pretty certain, but I didn't really get into it until I came to New York last week."

"Stay here," I said. "Don't go away. Look, Peter, I can get you a scholarship to this really great prep school. It'll be a good college after that. You're smart," I said. "I can tell. I'll do it, Peter, if you stay. I promise you that, Peter."

"I got straight As in school, Bruce, but I don't

want to go back. I want all the things I never had. I want to be rich, Bruce."

"Don't go Peter. Don't leave. It's a bad scene. We want you to stay. Think about it, overnight, at least."

He smiled at me. A very sad, knowing, direct-in-my-eyes smile. He didn't look away.

"Don't feel bad, Bruce. It's okay. I want to do it."

"When it turns sour, Peter, come back. If you ever get in trouble, call me. If you need a place to hide, my number is in the book. Any time. Until you come back I'll miss you. . ." I had to stop. It was getting pretty hard for me to go on.

"Thanks," he said. "I'm glad you care about me."

"I do," I said. "A lot."

"I've got to split, Bruce. I told this guy I'd meet him at six. I'm staying at his place. Apt 46B, Bruce. It's on the 46th floor. It's got a great view of the city, Bruce. He's going to buy me some new clothes tomorrow. . ." His voice trailed off.

"I never knew my father, Bruce," he said suddenly.

He stood up abruptly, and for the first time his composure deserted him.

"Good-bye," he said.

"Good-bye," I said.

"Can I hug you?" he said.

"Sure," I said.

We hugged each other hard.

P.S. Peter will come back. I know he will. He just doesn't understand yet. He wants many things too much and he wants, needs, just one person to care about him.

He's only 16 — a young 16, and he's a good kid. You shouldn't think he's not.

It's really important for us to be here when the Peters come back. Older, sadder, wiser. He'll remember the hug.

CONCLUSION

While We Have Time, Let Us Do Good

Underlying every great and noble work is a very simple vision of what that work is. The vision of Covenant House is quite simply this: Kids should not be bought and sold. They should not be exploited. It should not be infinitely dangerous to be alone and homeless on the streets of our cities. There must be a place where they can all get help. And when they need it: before it's too late. And from people who love and respect them. With no strings. No questions asked. And in a place where nobody gets excluded. That's what "catholic" is supposed to mean.

"Catholic" is supposed to mean universal. "Catholic" is supposed to mean nobody is excluded.

Jesus had a hard time making that point. He still does.

Just about all his friends — and certainly most of His enemies — wanted to make Jesus sectarian.

His friends and His enemies alike didn't want Him to associate with lepers or Samaritans, or publicans or sinners — or even women.

The disciples of John and Jesus had their own turf battles over who were greater. And everybody thought it was okay to hate the Romans.

If you want to hate somebody, or to exclude them from your company, or make yourself better than they are, you can always find some religious, economic, cultural, ethnic, or historical reason to do so.

When Jesus finally — with some impatience, I think — taught us who was going to make it into His kingdom, he did so without reference to doctrinal or sectarian conditions.

He said very clearly that it was mercy, not doctrine; pity, not dogma; love, not credal statements that got you into His company. He said we are welcome into His kingdom if we feed the hungry, clothe the naked, shelter the homeless, comfort the afflicted. And if we don't do these things, we're not welcome.

Far too often, well-meaning men and women have tried to exclude others from their love on the basis of doctrine or race or money or sexual orientation — or for dozens of other reasons.

We make ourselves uncatholic that way.

Love doesn't exclude anybody.

God is nonsectarian.

So is Covenant House. We are proud to be an agency that strives very hard never to become uncatholic.

Nobody gets turned away.

It is a matter of promises to keep. To you, to my kids. To God.

When all is said and done, there aren't many good reasons for doing good.

For some of us, the good itself is sufficient reason. For others, it is the simple need of good and brave and beautiful kids who sometimes have lost even the ability to inspire our pity.

Others perhaps look beyond the goodness of the simple deed, and beyond the goodness of the kids themselves, to a perfect and compelling goodness they find in God alone.

I really don't think it matters very much to God, who is quite above our need to praise Him for the good we should do.

However, and whyever, we are led or drawn or choose to do good for the kids who need us, it is enough that we do it.

It means a lot if we do it for love.

St. Francis, at the end of his life, left one simple injunction for his friends: *Dum tempus habemus, operemur bonum!* Brothers and Sisters, while we have time, let us do good.

EPILOGUE

Observations
and Suggestions

1. *Kids should not be bought and sold. Kids should not he exploited. Sex is not a commodity and a kid is not merchandise. Nobody is. If you buy a girl on the street, you have to know she is owned by a pimp. You pay, but so does she — an awful price. The pimp gets rich. On the other hand, a boy free lances. He's just lonelier, and he dies sooner.*

2. *Sex was never supposed to be a spectator sport. When did we ever think that voyeurs and exhibitionists were "normal?" You don't need to watch that porno film. Those "respectable" skin magazines are not what healthy sex is all about. Don't buy them and the publishers will go out of business. Simple. Boycott your local video dealer if he rents hard-core porn. Almost all do.*

3. *Reach out to a hurting kid. You can't save the world. Nobody can. But you can save a kid's life. Be a catcher in the rye. . .*

4. *Start living by — if you don't already — some*

moral or ethical code that can make you proud
of yourself. Watch what you teach kids by your
lifestyle, by your words, by the values you live
by. . . Do you really want kids to believe in and
imitate what you think and do?

5. Sex isn't love and love isn't sex. It's good and
    beautiful when it's between married people who
    love each other and it's private. Teach your kids
    about sex and family and marriage. Do it early
    and often. Ask your churches to help if you
    aren't ready and willing. If you and your
    churches don't do it, don't object if our schools
    do!

6. Pick out some aspect of the problem of exploited
    kids and do something about it. Join or start a
    group. Five people working together accom-
    plish more than 100 individuals working alone.
    Become politically streetwise. There are no
    great mysteries about it: politicians respond to
    appropriate, persevering pressure. There are
    laws that need changing and laws that need
    passing, like making it illegal for a 16-year-old
    kid to make a porn film! In some states, like New
    York, it's still legal!

7. Urge your churches, synagogues and service
    clubs to address the plight of homeless and
    exploited kids. Even more: ask your pastors,
    rabbis and community leaders to address

thoughtfully the sexploitational attitudes encouraged and fostered by the media. What are your churches really doing for teenagers? Anything? See to it!

8. Somebody distributes and sells drugs; somebody else buys them. Both are equally responsible and equally guilty for the thousands of murders and payoffs and wasted kids. To what extent are we a part of that problem?

9. If you're a kid, DON'T run away. Call the Covenant House Nineline — 1-800-999-9999. It's a toll-free, 24-hour helpline. We can help! If you're a kid and have run away from home, DON'T stay on the street. JUST DON'T! Please. Call the Covenant House Nineline. Do it now. If you're a parent worried about your kid and need help, call the same number. We'll do our best to help you.

Dum tempus habemus, operemur bonum!

A Gift
to Be Embraced

Reflections on the
Covenant House Faith Community

The following was written by Alec Aspinwall, a member of the Covenant House Faith Community in New York City since January of 1988.

Even after making the decision to visit the Covenant House Faith Community in New York City, I have to admit I was still somewhat suspicious. The closer I got to the address on Eighth Avenue in the heart of Times Square, in fact, the more my questions grew. What would draw normal people away from their comfortable lifestyles to pray for three hours a day and work with street kids while making $12 a week? What was drawing me?

For some time I had been searching for a way to deepen my relationship with God, and there was certainly something pushing me to take a closer look. Now that courage seemed foolish and even a little frightening as I stood on the doorstep waiting for someone to answer the bell. I tried to look nonchalant, but as I glanced across the street, my eyes read the invitation posted on the door of the porno theatre and I turned away in disgust — but without success. All around me, as I looked to the left and then to the right, the sorry sights and sounds of a string of "adult entertainment centers" made my stomach turn. I felt stunned. Is this where I had to live if I wanted to feel closer to God? Was I crazy? The eyes of the street people told me what I already knew. "You don't belong here," they said. They were right. I didn't belong here.

Then the door opened, and I was met with a warm smile. I tried to contain my gratitude for the timely rescue.

Once inside I was surprised by the size of the dwelling. It consisted of two six-story buildings joined by a large chapel. The dormitory-style living was neither elegant nor impoverished, but quite plain. The people I was soon to meet, however, were anything but plain.

I found myself in the midst of a Christian "melting pot." There were nurses, teachers, nuns, businesspeople, laborers, retired mothers, and recent college graduates. They had come from all over the country and even from abroad. Although Catholic in prayer and worship, the Community also had members from various Christian denominations. There were conservatives and liberals, rich and not so rich, young and the young at heart. Each had a different story to tell as to why they had come to Covenant House, but their differences were united by the call to strengthen their relationship with one God. To do so, they were willing to accept the challenge of intense prayer (three hours a day), communal living, and working with the kids of Covenant House, whose lifestyle on the street can make them pretty tough to deal with at times. They hurt so much that sometimes the only way they can feel better about themselves is to hurt you instead.

I had also expected Community members to be a solemn bunch, bearing the weight of the pervasive tragedy that surrounded them — but I found just the opposite to be true. The Community had a vibrant spirit that was full of life and laughter. Somehow the pain they were daily exposed to had actually made room for joy. I'm not saying that I didn't perceive their own suffering, for many of them shared with me the struggles they were experiencing with the kids of Covenant House and with themselves. But they were beginning to see their struggle no longer as a punishment to be endured, but as a gift to be embraced. I began to think that there might be something to that line from the Gospel about how "dying to yourself will bring new life."

By the end of my week, I had a lot to think and pray about. Was I ready to commit to a minimum of 13 months of three hours a day of prayer? Could I dedicate myself to a simple lifestyle in a chaste community? Was I able to let go of the stability offered by my loved ones and my career? Was I willing to be sent to any one of the Covenant House sites assigned to me and work at any job, whether it was working directly with the kids or not? Most of all, could I really love those hardened street kids and let myself be touched by their pain?

I went home to California and asked God to give me a sign. Something simple. An eclipse maybe! No sign came. What did come, finally, was a sense of peace that told me it was alright to go against all the norms and ambitions ingrained in me and take a step forward in faith. After receiving a letter from the Orientation Director, I gave notice at my job and began to make plans to come back to New York.

It's hard to believe I've been here a year now. I've learned so much about myself, the kids, and God. I've learned, for instance, that drawing closer to God is a constant challenge and process. Street kids, I've come to learn, really have soft centers underneath those hard exteriors, and they often have more to teach me than I them. And God is always there, even though sometimes I don't recognize Him.

I still don't like the neighborhood, and I still get the same stares on the street that I did a year ago. Only now, sometimes I see Christ behind the cold eyes, and He reassures me, "You do belong here."

———————

If you would like more information about joining the Faith Community, please write to Pat Kennedy at Covenant House Faith Community, 460 W. 41st Street, New York, NY 10036, or call (212)-613-0331.

COVENANT HOUSE

How old do I have to be to join Covenant Community? Are married couples welcome?

Sometimes exceptions are made, but generally 22 is the minimum age we consider, and 65 the maximum age. Married couples who have no dependents and have been married for at least 18 months are welcome.

Why do you ask for a commitment of 13 months?

Because we ask for a year of service and one month of formation and preparation.

What costs will Community pay for?

Food, housing, health and life insurance along with a small weekly stipend is given. Surprisingly, most people find that they can live on $12 a week and have fun doing it.

What if I have student loans?

Student loans can be deferred up to three years.

Do I have to pray three hours a day? Is it really necessary?

Yes, prayer is non-negotiable; it's the root and reason for everything we're able to do here at Covenant House.

Do I have to be a Catholic to be accepted into the Community? Can I practice my own faith and still be a member?

You do not have to be Catholic. We welcome

people from diverse religious backgrounds, but we do follow the Roman Catholic order of worship service. However, individuals can attend their own church services on the weekend as well.

I want to work with your kids, but I have no experience in child care. Is there training available, or would I be put in a different area?

If you're really interested in working directly with the kids, we feel confident that we'll be able to help you learn how to work with our kids at Covenant House.

Will I know my particular job as well as where I'll be placed before I make a final commitment?

If you have a particular interest or background in serving Covenant House through a particular job or area, we'd give that special consideration. But we like to ask that you be open to serving wherever the need is.

Can I request placement at one of your foreign missions in Central America?

If you have an interest in applying for our Central America program, you must first serve for six months in Community stateside before going abroad.

"I bound myself by oath, I made a covenant with you . . . and you became mine."   **Ezekiel 16:8**

Sometimes God Has a Kid's Face is a collection of Father Bruce Ritter's newsletters recounting the remarkable history and mission of Covenant House. His entire collection of newsletters, *Covenant House: Lifeline to the Street*, is available on hardcover, published by Doubleday.

The only way to stop the pain and degradation of street children is to get more people involved in solutions to the devastating problems they face every night of their lives.

After you read this book, please pass it along to a friend. If you would like more copies, just fill out this coupon and return it to us. And know that because you took the time to care, a kid won't have to sell himself to survive tonight.

Please send me _____ copies of *Sometimes God Has a Kid's Face*. To help defray the cost of sending you these books, we request a minimum donation of $3 per book. Please allow 6-8 weeks for delivery.

Name _____

Address _____

City_____ State _____ Zip _____

Please make your check payable to Covenant House.
Your gift is tax deductible.

COVENANT HOUSE

JAF Box 2973
New York, NY 10116-2973

FKBDND

"I bound myself by oath, I made a covenant with you . . . and you became mine." **Ezekiel 16:8**

Covenant House depends almost entirely on gifts from friends like you to help over 25,000 homeless and runaway children every year. We provide food, clothing, shelter, medical attention, educational and vocational training and counseling to kids with no place to go for help. Please help if you can.

YES! I want to help kids at Covenant House. Here is my gift of:

$10 _____ $25 _____ $100 _____ Other _____

Name _____

Address _____

City _____ State _____ Zip _____

Please make your check payable to Covenant House.
Your gift is tax deductible.

COVENANT HOUSE
JAF Box 2973
New York, NY 10116-2973

FKAAND